Advance Praise for Forever A Foster Child

"*Forever A Foster Child: A Memoir of Resilience* is a deeply moving and unforgettable account of a woman's journey from a childhood born in chaos to a life forged through courage and hard-won strength. This powerful memoir is a true page-turner, revealing not only what it takes to survive but what it takes to heal and ultimately thrive.

Cynthia shares her story with striking honesty—growing up amid painful family dynamics, carrying the invisible wounds of her early years, and later facing a devastating divorce that nearly broke her. In those darkest moments, when everything she had built seemed to be falling apart, her resilience became her lifeline. Through heartbreak, loss, and profound disillusionment, she found the courage to rise again.

What emerges is the portrait of a woman with an iron will and a luminous spirit—someone who refused to let her past define her future. This book is not just a memoir; it is a testament to the power of the human spirit and a beacon of hope for anyone who has ever wondered whether they could begin again. Cynthia's story proves that even after life's deepest fractures, it is possible to rebuild, to heal, and to become more than you ever imagined."

—CHAR (CHARLOTTE) MURPHY, ESQ., 8x Bestselling Author, Creator and Curator of the Mission Hope International Bestselling Book Series

"*Forever A Foster Child* embraces the souls and hearts of readers from the beginning. Cynthia Goble shares her life's journey that would break many. It is her inner power, belief, drive, and inspiration that give readers hope that a better tomorrow does and can exist for one and all. The book is worthy of quiet time to comprehend all the words, thoughts, and realizations that nothing is impossible in this world when we have the drive and ambition to carry ourselves forward, no matter the outside chatter and barriers, to ultimately achieve what we hold close to heart and prove to ourselves that 'Yes I Can!'"

—ELINOR STUTZ, Smooth Sale, International Bestselling and Evergreen Author of *Nice Girls DO Get the Sale: Relationship Building that Gets Results*

"A powerful, heartfelt, emotional evoking testament to resilience and courage in the face of loss, abandonment, betrayal, and constant disruption in life. Eloquently written and formatted, the author finds connection and meaning through the love of her dogs and nature. The book inspires, uplifts, and gives hope to anyone who has undergone hard struggles due to unfortunate circumstances beyond their control."

—HARVEY DEUTSCHENDORF, speaker and Internationally Published Author of *The Other Kind of Smart: Simple Ways to Boost Your Emotional Intelligence for Greater Personal Effectiveness and Success* and *Emotional Intelligence Game Changers: 101 Simple Ways to Win at Work + Life.*

"*Forever A Foster Child* is a deeply human memoir—one that invites the reader not just to witness Cynthia Goble's life but to recognize themselves within it. This is not a story about surviving hardship alone; it is a mirror for anyone who has carried emotional trauma forward and learned, often quietly, how to remain intact.

Reading this book encouraged me to reflect on my own resilience and the ways I have navigated loss, instability, and emotional injury over time. Cynthia's honesty creates space for recognition rather than judgment, allowing the reader to see that resilience is not a single moment of triumph but a pattern formed through repetition, endurance, and self-awareness. I personally loved Chalay, as I had my own attachments growing up that felt stabilizing to me. Animals, mostly dogs, came later.

It took me a little longer to read than expected, particularly through the middle sections where emotional conditions repeat in ways that mirror real lived experience. While this repetition occasionally slowed my pace, it never detracted from the integrity or message of the story. In fact, it reinforced the reality of how trauma often revisits us in cycles. For that reason, I don't think it detracts from the book at all. It only reinforces the fact that we learn through continued experience and become more resilient from it.

Overall, this is a meaningful and courageous work—one that offers understanding rather than instruction, and recognition rather than resolution. I believe readers willing to engage with it openly will come away with a deeper understanding of themselves, their own resilience, and the quiet strength it takes to keep moving forward."

—BRIAN CURTIS, Author of *There Is Only One Heart*

"*Forever A Foster Child* is a tender and courageous journey through the landscapes of loss, resilience, and becoming. Even in the brief time I had to read sections of the manuscript, I was struck by the honesty of Cynthia's voice and the way she traces her experiences with such clarity and heart. Her reflections invite readers to sit with the complexities of growing up unseen, and to witness how strength can take shape in quiet, unexpected ways.

A deeply human story that will resonate with anyone who has ever carried wounds larger than their childhood."

—RUTH BRUNNER, Author of *Uniquely You: What If Your Difference Is Your Greatest Gift?*

"*Forever A Foster Child* is not a memoir that asks for attention; it offers presence. Cynthia Goble writes with rare emotional integrity. She does not sensationalize pain or rush healing. Instead, she invites the reader into a quiet, honest witnessing of a life shaped by displacement, resilience, and grace.

What stayed with me most was the spiritual undercurrent woven throughout her story—the awareness she carried as a child, the refuge she found in animals, the dignity of her father, and the quiet kindnesses that arrived when she needed them most.

This is a book about foster care, yes, but more deeply, it is a testament to resilience that does not harden the heart.

If you have ever felt unseen, displaced, or quietly strong, this book will meet you with tenderness and truth."

—ROHINI QURESHI, Author, eBook & Journal Designer, Trainer in Kindle Create & Self-Publishing, and Founder of Heart To Paper Gifts

"*Forever A Foster Child* reminds us that resilience is not just about enduring hardship but about reclaiming joy, connection, and the courage to thrive. Cynthia's story captures the strength it takes to survive instability, the comfort found in small acts of kindness, and the healing power of love, whether from a parent, a friend, or even the loyal companionship of animals. It is a memoir that speaks to anyone who has ever felt unseen, showing that resilience is as much about rebuilding and rediscovering ourselves as it is about survival."

—CARLENE HUTTON, Director / Founder of The Coaching Tribe International

"Cynthia Goble's memoir is a powerful and haunting exploration of the devastating impact addiction and family dysfunction can have on individuals and the entire family system. Her writing is both compelling and deeply insightful, especially in the way she captures the complex emotions that come with living in such an environment. I was particularly moved by her descriptive passages, which vividly illustrate the toll of trauma and the long journey toward healing."

— Lyn Sherman, MSW, LCSW (retired)

"A Soulful Testament to the Human Spirit – Through the Eyes of One Who Listens Deeply

Reading *Forever A Foster Child* felt like sitting in sacred space with a soul brave enough to bare its deepest truths. Cynthia Goble invites us into a story etched not only in trauma but in triumph—a life both disrupted and determined, disheartened yet divinely resilient.

As someone who's spent decades exploring the inner landscapes of self and soul, I found Cynthia's voice refreshingly unfiltered, profoundly human, and spiritually resonant. Her bond with nature and her canine companions speaks volumes about the universal yearning for connection and unconditional love. And in that, I saw not just her story but echoes of my own—and perhaps yours too.

What Cynthia does so well is alchemize pain into presence. She reminds us that our beginnings do not determine our becoming, and that in the wounds we often try to hide lies the very wisdom we're meant to share.

This book is not merely a memoir. It's a mirror, a light, a companion for the road. If you're navigating your own healing or seeking a deeper understanding of human resilience, Cynthia's journey is a gift. I highly recommend it—not just for what it says but for what it awakens."

—Zen Benefiel, MA, MBA, Author (40+ titles), Founder of Planetary Citizens

"*Forever A Foster Child* is not simply a memoir—it is a sacred offering. Cynthia doesn't just share memories, she holds up a mirror for every soul who has ever felt unheard, unseen, or unloved. Her resilience invites us to grieve, to feel, to remember, and most importantly, to hope. In walking through her journey, I discovered reflections of my own—and found the light beyond the pain. This book proves that even when life tries to break us, there is always a deeper strength waiting to build us back up. Thank you, Cynthia, for writing what so many are too afraid to say—and for reminding me of my own light."

—Dr. Dileep Kumar Mishra, Breath Code Creator

"Cynthia's narrative leaves the reader feeling that they are experiencing the journey themselves. A seasoned writer that delivers a heartfelt and compelling narrative that is gripping and honest. Her writing style paints a vivid picture and begs us to come along and understand what so many right in our midst endure and experience."

—Vincent Minichiello, PE, PMP

FOREVER
A FOSTER CHILD

A MEMOIR OF RESILIENCE

CYNTHIA GOBLE

BookJourney

Disclaimer

This memoir is a true account of the author's life. To protect the privacy of individuals involved, all names of people, locations, and institutions have been changed or fictionalized. Any resemblance to real persons, living or dead, or to actual places or organizations is purely coincidental. The breeds of the dogs mentioned are factual and have not been altered.

Dedication

To my father, Samuel Leonard Goble,
whose unwavering love, quiet strength, and unshakable belief in the power of education laid the foundation for my courage and resilience. Your wisdom continues to guide me, your strength sustains me, and your spirit lives on in every word of this story.

To Dr. Rachel Harris, PhD,
whose therapeutic guidance and boundless compassion extended far beyond the role of a professional. Even in retirement, your encouragement to share my story became a cornerstone of my healing and growth. I am forever grateful.

Table of Contents

Foreword

By Rachel Harris, PhD, author of *Swimming in the Sacred, Listening to Ayahuasca, Twenty Minute Retreats*, and coauthor of *Children Learn What They Live* and *Teenagers Learn What They Live*.

Forever A Foster Child is the story of one woman's life. It's a tale of profound deprivation, marital abuse, and survival or what Cynthia calls, resilience. I don't disagree with her theme of resilience; she is by far one of the most resilient people I have ever met. Underlying her theme of resilience is her desire to live, her existential choice to remain on this earthly realm. I don't mean she was ever suicidal. This was a spiritual decision.

Cynthia doesn't tell the story of when she walked into one of those libraries that were her refuge during her homeless years. A small child took one look at her and asked, "Are you an angel?" Out of the mouths of babes. Cynthia is not quite of this world, and this small stranger recognized that quality in her.

Despite her struggles, Cynthia was clear in her decision to remain in this life, on this planet, to survive and to contribute according to her deeply held ethical standards in a business world that typically stretches those standards. Although as highly competent as she describes herself, Cynthia did not really fit in the business world, a culture that called for Harvard Business School to create a course on ethics. I'm not sure how effective that course was, but that's a different story.

Cynthia's other lifelong calling is to care for the animals she loves so dearly. Starting with her beloved stuffed animal, Chalay, Cynthia breathed life into this early relationship. Chalay was more than just a favorite toy or imaginal friend. This little monkey was alive to her and a source of comfort and solace she so desperately needed as a young and seriously neglected child.

As her therapist, I have to admit it took me quite a while to understand how important this relationship with Chalay was in her life. The best thing I can say about my professional self is that I was smart enough to keep my mouth shut. I never questioned this early attachment to Chalay. I gradually came to understand that this relationship sustained her and was, perhaps, an early sign of her spiritual gifts. I believe Cynthia is right in her later life to connect the soldier who told her to "keep your head down" to her relationship with Chalay.

Both beings served the same purpose, to protect her when she needed it the most. Note: I use the term "beings" intentionally; they were alive to her.

Cynthia writes of her love for animals but not in a generalized way. She's specific about her relationships with her beloved dogs. And, of course, these are reciprocal relationships. Her dogs love her, too, and these relationships are a great healing in her life both psychologically and spiritually.

In all her relationships and all her experiences, Cynthia consistently reaches for the most positive influence possible. This is nowhere more important than with the devastating loss of her father, the most responsive and healthy person in her young life. I have to imagine that her father, who knew he was dying, intentionally encouraged Cynthia in the most practical of ways. As a final act of love, he told Cynthia to "go to college," which has served as a ticket out of what he must have known was a very dysfunctional family. The way he lived his too short life has served as an inspiration to Cynthia in terms of integrity, discipline, and hard work.

The villain in her story is her ex-not quite husband. I never met him but I agree with her portrayal. He was intentionally malicious in his disregard for her financial security and welfare. And Cynthia made the cultural mistake of that time in trusting him and allowing herself to become financially dependent. In this way, Cynthia is a symbol of how women were supposed to behave in the fifties and what she was taught as a child from the women in her family.

I would be remiss if I didn't acknowledge that I broke a clear professional code by not charging Cynthia for therapy. Supposedly if a client doesn't pay, they don't really value the therapy. This was never the case. I knew Cynthia appreciated my commitment to her. But my decision was on a different level. I viewed my work with Cynthia as part of my own spiritual job. I didn't completely understand this assignment or, for that matter, who assigned it, but I trusted and accepted the work order. I lived up to my spiritual calling in my work with Cynthia, and one way this manifested in the therapeutic relationship is that both Cynthia and I took her dreams and visions seriously and received guidance from them. In the midst of her struggles, her unfolding spiritual life served as a guiding light for our therapeutic process.

What can be learned from one woman's life? More than *just* resilience, Cynthia's life story is a lesson in trusting your inner self despite life's disappointments and challenges. This is the story within her story and an inspiration for all of us.

Introduction

Shattered Stillness: A Journey to Resilience

On March 22, 1998, the stillness before dawn carried no warning of the storm that would soon shatter everything I thought I knew. A dream, vivid and haunting, pulled me into a scene that felt all too real: Adam, my partner of twenty years, stood confident beside a young Asian woman and her child. His expression was warm, exuding a pride I hadn't seen in years—a painful contrast to the man who had grown cold and distant within our shared life.

When I awoke, unease lingered like a shadow. Dreams had always offered both comfort and warning, often blurring the line between the subconscious and the prophetic. By sunrise, that unease compelled me to act. Standing before Adam's briefcase, I uncovered the pieces of a hidden life: letters laced with affection that weren't mine, photographs capturing moments I was never meant to see, and receipts that painted a picture of betrayal. Each discovery cut deeper than the last, unraveling the trust I had nurtured over two decades.

The confrontation that followed was chilling and disappointing. Adam's dismissive tone, paired with a mechanical shrug, reduced our life together to an inconvenience he could no longer entertain. His indifference, sharper than any accusation, left me questioning our relationship and my sense of self. For someone who had already weathered the heartbreak of a tumultuous childhood, this betrayal felt like an impossible blow. The fragile foundation I had built around my adult life crumbled beneath me.

But this is not a story of surrender. It is about resilience—the quiet, determined strength that emerges in the aftermath of devastation. That morning, standing amid the ruins of a life I no longer recognized, I faced a choice: to remain shackled by betrayal or to reclaim my worth and forge a new path forward.

Resilience, I would learn, is not the ability to endure. It is the power to rebuild the lessons drawn from a childhood marked by instability and an adulthood tested by pain. In the darkest moments, it was small, deliberate acts—a tearful call to a therapist, reclaiming space in my home, finding solace in the loyalty of my dogs—that marked the beginning of my transformation.

Through this book, I invite you to walk with me through the wreckage, witness the rebuilding, and discover the essence of resilience: a strength born from vulnerability, honed by adversity, and nurtured through hope. This is not just my story—it is a testament to the resilience that lives within us all.

Letter to Readers

Dear Reader,

Welcome to *Forever A Foster Child: A Memoir of Resilience*. Thank you for choosing to embark on this journey with me. Writing this memoir has been a personal and transformative experience, and it is my hope that these pages will offer insight, encouragement, and perhaps even healing for those who need it most.

This is not a recounting of events but a testament to the power of resilience, hope, and the human spirit. My story—from a tumultuous childhood marked by uncertainty, to finding my voice and purpose—is one of navigating challenges that many may find unimaginable. Yet, it is also a story of triumph, of breaking generational cycles, and of discovering that our greatest strength often lies within us, waiting to be uncovered.

While this memoir is rooted in my personal experiences, it is also written with you in mind. Whether you are someone who has walked a similar path, a foster parent, a social worker, or a compassionate soul seeking to understand, I want you to know that you are not alone. The lessons I have learned and the resilience I have cultivated are not unique to me; they are universal truths that can be embraced and shared.

This book is not about dwelling on the pain of the past but about shining a light on the possibilities of the future. It is about the importance of kindness, self-discovery, and the courage to dream beyond the boundaries that life may impose. It is about breaking cycles, finding hope in the darkest moments, and realizing that resilience is more than survival—it is about thriving.

As you turn these pages, I hope you will find moments that resonate with you, challenge you, and inspire you. More than anything, I hope you find a renewed sense of hope and empowerment. We all have the capacity to rise above our circumstances and create a life filled with purpose and joy.

Thank you for allowing me to share my story with you. I invite you to read with an open heart, and I encourage you to reflect on your own journey as you do. Together, let us celebrate the strength and beauty of the human spirit.

With gratitude and hope,

Cynthia Goble

Prologue

Light Before the Storm

Long before the world tried to define me—before the bruises, the silence, the longing for belonging—I knew who I was.

I am Light from Light.

As a very young child, lying on my twin-sized bed, I would drift into a state beyond dreams. In those sacred, suspended moments, I was no longer bound by my body. I was not a little girl in a home. I was not afraid. I was not alone. I was pure, radiant consciousness, shimmering in a field of luminous gold, untouched by time.

I belonged to something vast and eternal.

In that place, I did not need words. There was no hunger or fear. There was no before or after. I could see in all directions, not with eyes but with knowing. I was part of the universe's pulse, woven into the fabric of everything. I was Home.

And then, I wasn't.

I remember being in a bassinet carriage, one of many in a softly lit nursery. I recall watching—curious, not frightened—as the light dimmed and the veil of earthly life settled over me. There was a brief pause, a sacred hesitation. But eventually, I agreed to come. I said yes.

Later, as a toddler, I asked my mother whether people aged backward. I was sure we must be returning from something divine. Her answers didn't match the truth I carried inside me, the truth I remembered. So I learned not to ask again. I held my wonder quietly. I buried my Light.

People called me quiet, introspective, strange even—but they didn't know I was guarding a secret: that I had once been more than this.

And then the world tried to erase that knowing.

Foster care. Abuse. Loss. A system that chewed through innocence. I became just another statistic. Another misplaced child with questions too big for the grown-ups around her.

But still, the Light didn't leave me. It flickered beneath the surface, waiting. Even in my darkest hours—when trust was shattered and the idea of "home" became a phantom—I never forgot where I came from. That memory, that truth, became my compass.

This is not a story of despair. This is a story of return.

Of remembering.

Of reclaiming the Light that was nearly extinguished by the world's weight. This is a journey through the shattered pieces of childhood toward something whole. It is about what happens when the soul refuses to be silenced—when we choose, again and again, to believe in healing, in spirit, in self.

Before I was anything else, I was Light.

And so, I begin this story where all stories truly begin—not with trauma but with truth.

Part I

The Fragile Years

Chapter 1
Through Innocent Eyes

I WAS BORN IN A CITY along the South Texas shoreline, where the breezy gulf air and coastal charm shaped my earliest memories. On Christmas Eve of 1952, I entered the world as a hazel-eyed baby with light strawberry blonde hair—a unique feature that captivated my father's English-Scottish family. Weighing in at eight pounds, ten ounces, my arrival seemed full of promise.

But joy quickly turned to fear. Within hours, complications arose—a digestive reaction to infant formula that left the obstetrician certain my days were numbered. My family took turns holding me, cherishing what they feared might be fleeting moments.

Against all odds, I survived. Looking back, I now see this as the first of many challenges that would teach me resilience—and how to defy the obstacles placed in my path.

In those years, my childhood home was a mix of warmth, curiosity, and the security my father provided. He was my rock, a steady presence whose dreams for me were rooted in love and aspiration. He envisioned a future where I would excel in my education, find a stable career, and build a life of happiness. My mother, though nurturing at times, was a more unpredictable figure, often consumed by her own struggles. Her emotional absence left me yearning for the encouragement I needed.

My paternal grandmother, Ivy, whom everyone called Nanny, adhered to traditional Southern values. She imagined a life for me centered on marriage and homemaking, aligning with the societal norms of the time. Yet, even as a young girl, I felt a quiet but firm determination to chart my own course. By first grade, I had already decided I would go to college—a dream that defied the expectations placed on me and hinted at my growing independence.

My father's roots trace back to a small town south of Dallas, where he was born into a middle-class family during the 1920s. It was a time when stability and tradition defined much of rural life. His father worked to provide for his family, while his mother managed the household. Education was valued, and my father excelled in public school, finding joy in the simple pleasures of the time, like radio and movies.

The Great Depression shattered that sense of stability, prompting the family to relocate to the Texas Gulf Coast in search of better opportunities. My father's life took another dramatic turn with the bombing of Pearl Harbor in 1941. At sixteen, he joined the US Navy in 1946, serving in the South Pacific. When his father died the following year, my father received an honorable discharge to return home and care for his grieving mother and older sister.

By contrast, my mother's upbringing in South Texas was marked by far greater turbulence. Raised by uneducated parents, her family dynamic revolved around her grandmother, an immigrant from the Czech Republic who spoke no English. Appearances were paramount in her family, with her parents insisting she dress well to attract a husband. My mother had struggled to graduate from high school and battled severe, untreated mental health challenges, including anorexia and bulimia—issues that were not understood at the time. Her struggles extended into adulthood, manifesting as manipulative behaviors, prescription drug dependency, and lasting health complications, including pancreatitis.

The shadows of the Great Depression and the upheaval of World War II loomed over both my parents' lives. Economic instability defined those years, and while the post-war boom offered new opportunities, they were not without sacrifices. My parents married in 1950 and began their family soon after. My eldest sister, Sally, was born in 1951, followed by me on that fateful Christmas Eve in 1952, and my younger sister, Paulette, whom my family called Paulie, in 1957. Thanks to the GI Bill, my parents achieved the milestone of purchasing their first home in 1954—a proud moment that marked the start of our life as a growing family.

Family dynamics were influenced by my parents' relationships with their own families. My father was devoted to his parents. He mourned his father's passing, treasuring his clothing and other keepsakes as sentimental relics.

Nanny played a central role in our lives, hosting family meals and sharing common interests with my father, such as gardening, orchid cultivation, and photography.

Nanny often insisted that my parents' marriage should be annulled due to my mother's mental incompetence at the time of their union. I was too young to grasp the meaning of these conversations, but the anger they ignited between my mother and Nanny was unmistakable. Their arguments would escalate, filling the house with tension and leaving me unsettled. As a child, I sought escape in the quiet of our backyard away from my mother and Nanny's clashes.

My father's relationship with his in-laws was distant. He never spoke of my maternal grandfather, and his connection with my grandmother, Eva, remained polite but minimal. Cultural and language barriers created a quiet divide: Eva, who spoke Czech, represented a world my father neither understood nor attempted to bridge.

My mother's relationships were far more complicated. She leaned on Eva for emotional support, often neglecting us children to spend hours on the phone with her. Her dynamic with Nanny, however, was fraught with conflict. Religion was often at the center of their disputes. My mother's Catholic upbringing clashed with my father's Protestant background. Nanny's father had been a Protestant minister in England, and she carried an ingrained tendency to preach. These religious differences would erupt into loud arguments that reverberated through the house, turning it into a battleground of beliefs.

Through these experiences, I began to see the contradictions that shaped my family and the world around me. My father's ambitions for my future stood in stark contrast to my mother's ambiguity about what lay ahead for me. The tension, though heavy, fueled my resolve. I was determined to forge my own path—one shaped by an unshakable belief in the possibility of something more.

From the very beginning, two profound forces shaped my existence: a connection to the spiritual realm and an innate bond with animals. These gifts set me apart, offering companionship and understanding that no human ever seemed to match.

As a young child, I experienced moments that felt like dreams yet carried a depth beyond imagination. Lying in my twin-sized bed in the room I shared with Sally, I drifted into ethereal encounters that transcended time and space.

In those moments, I returned to a realm where I existed as pure Light, unbound by a physical body. There, I was free—untouched by fear, pain, or material concerns—part of something greater, woven into the very fabric of existence. I saw without eyes, understood without words, and felt a belonging no other experience could replicate.

Before my birth, I hesitated, lingering in the space between worlds before consenting to this human form. One of my earliest memories was lying in a bassinet carriage, surrounded by other infants in a warm lit room. I contemplated my surroundings, feeling both present and distant, before drifting back to sleep.

Unlike other children, who seemed rooted in the tangible realities of childhood, I carried this awareness with me always. My intuition led me to question the world in ways others did not. Once, I asked my mother if people aged backward, sensing a truth beyond what she could explain. She answered, "When you grow up, you'll see that you were young and then became old." Her words didn't resonate with me. I held firm to what I knew deep inside.

I learned that my spirituality was not something to be shared. It was a quiet part of me, something I cherished and protected. People described me as reserved, but I was guarding the sacred knowledge of who I was and where I had come from before stepping into this life on Earth. What I couldn't have known then was that these gifts—this connection to something beyond—would become my greatest source of strength through life's most unpredictable and difficult moments.

Alongside my spiritual awareness, my love for animals became a defining part of me. Unlike people, animals never dismissed what they couldn't understand.

Midnight, a feral black cat with piercing green eyes, would glide into our backyard, allowing the briefest touch before vanishing into the night. She was a mystery, a fleeting presence that left me longing for her return.

My first pet—a guinea pig gifted to me when I was three—brought me immeasurable joy. Its soft fur and gentle squeaks filled my tiny world with delight. Then, one morning, I found it lifeless in its cage. My mother's harsh reaction, blaming me for its death, made my grief even heavier. I was too young to carry such blame, yet I bore it, nonetheless. Though I didn't have the words for it then, I understood that love and loss were always intertwined.

Not all my experiences with animals were marked by sorrow. One of my most cherished companions was a rooster—a bold, spirited creature whose crowing was music to my ears, though less so to the neighbors. I admired him. Then, one day, he was gone. My mother dismissed my questions with a cold, final explanation: "The neighbors complained." But her words did nothing to soothe the ache of his absence. His abrupt disappearance left an emptiness I couldn't express, teaching me another lesson about the unpredictability of life.

Even fleeting encounters with animals left a lasting imprint on my heart. One unforgettable Saturday at the park, Sally and I met a playful dog whose wagging tail and trusting eyes made us feel as if we had known him forever. We ran and played together, forming a bond that felt timeless, even though it lasted a few hours. When it was time to leave, we begged our parents to let us take him home. They refused, reasoning that he must belong to someone. As we drove away, the dog chased after our car, his silhouette shrinking in the rearview mirror. I wanted to plead with my father to stop, but I knew my mother would object. Tears streamed down my face as I realized I would never see him again.

Again and again, animals entered my life, bringing love, joy, and companionship—to leave too soon. Each encounter reinforced a bittersweet truth: Love is beautiful.

Of all the animals that fascinated me, none captured my heart more than the bloodhound. Their droopy eyes, long ears, and soulful expressions left a deep and lasting impression. One bright afternoon in Texas, Sally and I were playing outside when I spotted a bloodhound across the street. Without hesitation, I broke my parents' rule about crossing alone and ran straight to the dog. As I wrapped my arms around its massive frame, a profound feeling washed over me—an unflinching connection, as if I had always known this breed. When the owner confirmed it was a bloodhound, I declared with absolute certainty, "When I grow up, I'm going to have a dog just like this."

I never saw that particular bloodhound again, but that moment planted a seed in my heart. Even as a child, I knew these loyal, soulful dogs would be part of my life. It wasn't a fleeting childhood fascination—it was something deeper, something meant to be.

These two forces—my spirituality and my love for animals—became my guideposts, offering me both direction and solace. In a world that often felt unpredictable, they remained constant, shaping not who I was but who I would become. Through every loss, every unspoken connection, and every moment of intuitive knowing, they reminded me that I was never alone.

On my fourth birthday, I received a gift that would change my young life: a stuffed chimpanzee toy. Measuring about twenty-one inches tall, he had a soft plush body and a vinyl face, ears, hands, and shoes. His suspenders jingled with bells, and a red satin bow adorned his neck. A yellow vinyl banana, peeled just enough to reveal its fruit, was gripped in his right hand. His lips, a bright red tongue, and dark eyes seemed to understand my deepest thoughts. I named him Chalay, though I didn't know why. The name came to me in an instant, as certain and unshakable as the rising sun or the steady rhythm of my own heartbeat. Chalay became my constant companion, my anchor in an unpredictable world. I thought he would be with me forever.

I remember the moment I discovered his name, a truth that settled into my chest like an answered prayer. When I told my parents, my mother asked if I meant "Charlie." I shook my head. "No, he said his name is Chalay." My father teased me, calling him "Chalay the Chimpanzee," but their laughter did not shake my certainty. I knew him in a way no one else could.

As a child, loneliness was a familiar ache. Sally, often drowsy from her asthma medication, drifted between wakefulness and sleep, leaving me without a playmate. Eva watched over me while my parents worked, a distant figure in my life, more like a shadow than a source of comfort. She spoke little English, but her silence was not one of tenderness; it was thick with avoidance, her breath carrying the sharp sting of alcohol. I begged my mother to stay home with me, but her explanations were always the same—work was necessary, money was tight, and there were bills to pay. I did not yet understand the mounting hospital bills that shackled both my parents to their jobs.

And so, I turned to Chalay. His long arms and legs wrapped around me when sadness crept in, his ever-present gaze assuring me that I was loved. He was my guardian, my secret-keeper, my solace in a world that often felt too vast, too cold.

During visits to my paternal grandparents' home in a small western suburb of our city, I explored Nanny and Pappy's lush greenhouses filled with award-winning orchids, their delicate petals brushing against my fingertips like whispered secrets. I was mesmerized by the history of our family's ancestry, yet none of it comforted me the way Chalay did. He was always there, his silent companionship far more meaningful than any family legacy.

Then, one day, I lost him.

It happened on the drive home from Nanny's house. A sudden, hollow realization struck my chest like a stone dropped into deep water. "Chalay!" I cried out, my voice trembling with panic. My father pulled the car to the side of the road and turned back, his voice steady, assuring me that we would find him. When we arrived, Nanny greeted us at the door, Chalay cradled in her arms. "I knew you'd come back," she said. Relief surged through me, but so did embarrassment. How could a stuffed toy hold such power over me? And yet, he did.

But Chalay was never meant to stay forever.

On a warm summer day, a year and a half after receiving Chalay, the unthinkable happened. I had taken Chalay outside to the garage while Sally and I played. My pet rabbit, a gift from my parents for Easter, had grown fast, his once-tiny paws now strong and sure. As always, I reached into his wooden crate to pet him before heading inside for lunch. When we returned, the air was still, heavy with an unspoken tragedy. Chalay lay crumpled on the ground near the rabbit's enclosure, his bright red tongue torn open, stuffing spilling like lifeblood from his mouth.

I screamed.

Grief crashed into me, a tidal wave of horror and guilt. My rabbit had chewed through his fabric body, his innocent curiosity shattering the constant in my life. I clutched Chalay's limp form, but he was no longer there. The soul I had believed in, the presence that had watched over me, was gone. And it was my fault. I had been careless. I had failed him.

I never saw Chalay again. My parents tried to replace him, but there was no other like him. The store shelves were filled with imitations, lifeless and unfamiliar. In my heart, I knew the truth—he was irreplaceable. His absence left a hollow ache that never faded or dulled with time.

Years later, I would come to understand that Chalay's loss had been a cruel prelude, a lesson in impermanence. Three years after his "death," my father was diagnosed with terminal cancer. Overnight, my childhood was stripped from me. I had no time to mourn toys or play pretend. I watched the man who had carried me on his shoulders wither before my eyes, and when he was gone, the grief was unbearable. But in some small, aching way, I had already learned how to endure the unthinkable.

Chalay had been my first heartbreak, my first taste of irretrievable loss. Even now, I hold his memory close, a quiet testament to the love and resilience that carried me through the darkest moments of my life. Perhaps, in some way, he was always meant to be my guardian angel in disguise.

One of my favorite toys growing up was a puzzle board of the United States. Each piece, sturdy and vibrant, unlocked a world of curiosity and wonder. Sally and I spent hours fitting the pieces together, learning the names and locations of the states.

California captivated me the most. Its sprawling shape and western location made it a symbol of magic—Disneyland. When my dad traveled to San Francisco and Los Angeles for employment training seminars, he brought back Musketeer hats and other souvenirs for us, cementing my love for the state.

New York and New Jersey were trickier to place. I often confused their borders, but the challenge taught me patience and precision. I had a strong feeling that these two states would one day play a significant role in my life— and eventually, they did.

By second grade, I began to understand how different I was from my peers. My fair complexion, freckled skin, and hazel eyes made me stand out in ways I wished they wouldn't. My mother insisted on cutting my hair far shorter than I wanted, leaving me feeling betrayed. When a teacher mocked me, calling me a "plucked chicken," my humiliation deepened. From that day on, I vowed to grow my hair long, reclaiming a piece of myself.

My height made me an easy target for cruel nicknames like "Carrot Top," while my mother's struggles with undiagnosed anorexia cast another shadow over my childhood. As she fainted from malnourishment, she overfed me. I ate—not out of hunger but as part of an unspoken bargain. I wasn't seeking nourishment; I was trying to be good, hoping obedience might finally make me worthy of her love. At school and in my neighborhood, I felt trapped in a twisted fairytale—a modern-day Cinderella waiting for rescue.

Yet even in the midst of hardship, there were moments of light. Nanny filled my world with magic, sewing matching ruffled dresses for Sally and me. Her desserts—angel food cake, butter pound cake, and fruitcake steeped in brandy—were more than sweets; they were traditions, infused with love.

Chapter 2

The Day Everything Changed

∞

MY DAD EMBODIED integrity and love. One Saturday, he found a twenty-dollar bill in a stray shopping cart at a food market. Instead of keeping the money, he turned it in. Weeks later, when no one claimed it, the store returned it to him. He used the unexpected windfall to enrich our lives—buying necessities, installing a basketball hoop, and setting up a backyard pool for the hot Texas summers.

My dad's quiet gestures—holding my hand, resting an arm around my shoulder—spoke volumes about his love. But his influence extended far beyond those small, reassuring touches; it was woven into the way he carried himself every day. His parents and navy training instilled in him a strong sense of discipline, a deep respect for others, a belief in the transformative power of kindness, and the habit of always saying "please" and "thank you." He upheld a high standard of politeness and consideration, not out of obligation but because he understood the impact it had on those around him. From my earliest days, I watched how he treated everyone with dignity, how he made people feel valued. That standard became my own, a guiding principle that remained with me even through life's most difficult moments, when joy and purpose felt distant.

Beyond his interactions with people, my father instilled in me a respect for everything I had. Whether it was repairing our home, appliances, or tending to the garden, he reinforced the idea that respect wasn't just about how we treated others—it was a way of engaging with the world. Through his actions, he left a legacy of honesty, compassion, and purpose. His lessons continue to shape me, reminding me that true strength lies in living with integrity, kindness, and respect.

That sense of duty and respect for others wasn't just something he believed—it guided the most difficult choices of his life. Long before I was born, my family had already begun to fracture. My grandfather's sudden death from a heart attack during World War II left my father, then serving in the navy, torn between his military duty and the responsibility of supporting his widowed mother and older sister, Dorothy. Though he was devoted to his naval career, he made the painful decision to leave it behind, prioritizing his grieving family—a selfless act that shaped the course of our lives.

Years later, Aunt Dorothy confided that my father's decision to enlist had strained his relationship with my grandfather. Determined to serve his country, my father had lied about his age to join the navy, sacrificing his education and showing immense maturity for someone so young. Though his time in the military was brief, the ripples of his choices—both the enlistment and his sacrifice to return home—would resonate through our family for decades.

After his military service, my father brought his discipline and determination into civilian life, securing a coveted position at the southwestern regional office of the telephone company—one of the most respected employers of its time. Known for its stability, competitive benefits, and technological innovation, the company offered more than a job—it offered a future. By day, he worked in the high-security electronic switch room, where precision and reliability were paramount. By night, he attended high school classes to earn his diploma, driven by a quiet resolve to rise through the ranks. His perseverance was rewarded with a promotion to supervisor—a proud milestone for our family, marked with laughter when I, still young and learning, misheard "salary" as "celery."

With his promotion, my father dreamed of the perfect family home. In his free time, he searched for houses, drawn in particular to a two-story home by the marina that we had toured together. It offered a breathtaking view of the water, a spacious backyard, and a private dock that seemed to call to him. Owning a boat had always been his dream—a place to fish, relax, and share adventures with family and friends—and this home made that vision feel within reach.

He pictured sunny afternoons filled with boat rides, the laughter of loved ones echoing from the deck as he stood at the grill, barbecue sizzling in the salty air. He saw himself hand-cranking homemade ice cream on warm summer nights, the rhythmic turning of the handle accompanied by excited chatter as we awaited the first scoop. This home wasn't just a house—it was a promise of a life filled with joy, togetherness, and new beginnings.

Starting third grade at a new school didn't bother me. I had never struggled to make friends, and the prospect of a fresh start excited me. As I listened to my father describe the adventures we would have, I could already picture it all—the dock, the boat rides, the scent of barbecue in the air. It was more than his dream; it became mine too.

But life had other plans—harsh and unyielding. What my father initially brushed off as stress-induced back pain turned out to be something far more insidious: a malignant tumor near his spine. At just twenty-nine years old, he was given a devastating prognosis—three months to live. But in true defiance of the odds, he held on, not for months but for three more years. It was a testament to his unbreakable will, his deep-rooted faith, and the sheer force of his love for us. Every day was a battle—his body wasting away, pain relentless—but he fought on. The disease stripped away his strength, leaving him paralyzed from the waist down, his hands and arms weakening with time. His hair had fallen out, and his once-strong frame was reduced to little more than skin and bone.

The suffering was unimaginable. I can still see the bed sores that covered his fragile hips, the raw, open wounds so deep that his bones protruded through the bloody flesh. The holes drilled into his skull to drain fluid from his brain were haunting, a stark reminder of how merciless his illness was. And yet, through all of it, he never surrendered to despair. He cried out to God, not in defeat but in hope—for relief, for another day, for meaning in his suffering.

Looking back, I realize now that his fight, his resilience, shaped me in ways I could never have understood as a child. His suffering taught me to cherish life in a way many never do. While others dread another birthday, fearing the passage of time, I celebrate. Every year, every candle on the cake is a gift—one my father was denied too soon. I rejoice in my health, in the privilege of aging, because I know what it means to fight for every single day.

In 1959, at the age of seven, I was thrust into a world I wasn't prepared for, stepping into the role of caregiver while my father remained at home. I tended to his surgical wounds with shaky hands, emptied urine bottles, and sat with him in quiet moments, doing my best to offer him comfort.

Today, it's rare for an employer to take an active role in an employee's medical care, but in 1959, such support was not uncommon. At a time when medical insurance and employer-provided benefits were different from what they are today, this gesture lifted an immense burden from our family. Their generosity meant we had one less battle to fight, allowing us to focus on holding things together at home rather than struggling to navigate his treatment alone. Knowing his employer stood by him made all the difference.

My dad had been in and out of the hospital for months. When he was back home, his bedroom no longer looked the same. His regular bed had been replaced with a hospital bed, its cold metal railings a stark reminder of his fragile state. A patient lift with a sling stood nearby, a silent testament to how much his condition had worsened. My mother had given up their bed, sleeping instead on the small sofa in our tiny family room. On one particular night, the house was cloaked in an eerie stillness, pressing down on everything.

I was startled awake by the soft but insistent sound of my father's voice breaking through the silence. "Lala?" he called, summoning my mother with the name he always used with affection. A long pause followed, the stillness returning as though the house itself held its breath. When no response came, he called again, this time for my older sister. "Sally?" His voice carried both hope and quiet desperation.

Another stretch of silence, longer than the first, filled the space—a silence that seemed to stretch time itself. Then, he called my name, his tone questioning and weary. "Cindy?"

Something in his voice compelled me to answer. Before I knew it, I was standing beside his bed. The red travel alarm clock on the side table read 2:00 a.m. His face lit up with surprise as he asked if I could find him something to eat.

The hallway felt longer than usual as I walked toward the kitchen. The refrigerator offered a few options: leftover roast beef, a loaf of bread, and some cheese. I assembled a simple sandwich with roast beef and a light spread of mayonnaise.

When I returned, his gaze softened. He set the sandwich aside and asked me to stay. "Cindy," he said, "I need you to listen to me. I'm very sick. I'm not going to live much longer." His words landed like stones in my chest, and tears streamed down my face. Fear clouded my mind, but I clung to every word.

"You're not a little girl anymore," he continued. "You can take care of yourself. Focus on your studies, work hard, and one day, you'll have a good life." His message was meant to empower me, but it felt impossible. I trembled under the weight of his words, feeling both numb and aware of every moment.

He insisted I return to bed so I could go to school in the morning. As I lay in the darkness, his words echoed in my mind. I vowed to keep our conversation a secret, even from Sally and my mother. That night marked the end of my childhood and the beginning of an adulthood I wasn't ready for.

That night shaped me in ways I couldn't comprehend at the time. My dad's honesty and courage taught me more about resilience and spirituality than any lesson since. His words became the foundation for the life I built in his absence.

Some might say it was too much for a child to bear, and perhaps they'd be right. But I've never seen it that way. His honesty, though painful, was a gift. It prepared me for the storms ahead and gave me strength to navigate a lonelier world. Without that moment, I would have been lost when he passed.

Even now, I sometimes wish I had been calm enough to absorb more of his wisdom—how to navigate adulthood, choose a partner, or raise children. Yet, in our brief time, he gave me something far more enduring: values that have guided me through life.

My father's love and courage remain with me, embedded in the fabric of who I am. His strength, his belief in me, and his lessons in those fleeting moments form the foundation of my life. Decades later, I can still hear his voice, his words a lighthouse on a stormy shore, guiding me along a path he entrusted to me. His legacy is not one of loss but of love—a reminder that even in life's greatest challenges, there is strength and hope.

Chapter 3

A New World

$$\infty$$

THE THREE YEARS my father spent in the hospital felt like an eternity of uncertainty and heartache. Time lost meaning—days stretched into weeks, weeks blurred into months, and years passed without relief. Every moment was suspended in a void, an endless limbo where certainty was the ache of not knowing what would come next. I carried that weight everywhere, a silent burden lodged in my chest, making it hard to breathe.

Worry consumed me, sinking its teeth deeper with each passing day. It wrapped around my thoughts like an iron grip, tightening when I least expected it—when I sat in a classroom, unable to focus, or when I lay awake in the dark, my body trembling with exhaustion while my mind raced with dread. Where would I sleep next? How long would I be allowed to stay? Would I ever see my parents again? The questions circled in an endless loop, carving grooves of anxiety into my heart.

Even in a room full of children, even at a dinner table with adults who provided a roof over my head, I was alone. Their conversations drifted past me—words without warmth, without connection. Laughter sounded foreign, a language I no longer understood. The loneliness was a living thing, pressing against me, making every space feel smaller, every interaction hollow. I existed among others, but I was never with them.

Then came the flashbacks—brief, cruel glimpses of a life that no longer existed. My father's voice, steady and sure, guiding me through my schoolwork. The excitement of family vacations, filled with laughter and adventure. The simple comfort of sitting together at the dinner table, sharing stories and feeling safe. These memories arrived without warning, vivid and intoxicating, to vanish, leaving behind an unbearable ache. They were ghosts of happiness, haunting me when I least expected it.

My confidence crumbled under the weight of it all. I couldn't concentrate in school—words blurred together, numbers lost meaning, and my mind refused to stay in the present. Every attempt to focus was derailed by the relentless thoughts of survival. I felt myself slipping away, an observer in my own life, unable to grasp anything solid. I wanted to be seen, to be heard, to be held—but most of all, I wanted to go home. Yet home was no longer a place I could find. It existed in my memories, in the echoes of a life that had unraveled beyond repair.

When my father's doctors had done all they could, it wasn't a cold, corporate decision that led to his transfer to an oncology hospital in Houston—it was an extraordinary act of loyalty and compassion by the telephone company. They arranged everything, moving swiftly to give him a fighting chance.

It all happened so fast. My father had been ill for months before specialists in Houston took over his care, doing everything they could to save him from cancer. My mother stayed faithfully by his side, but her own health began to fail. A flare-up of her pancreatitis landed her in a different hospital, not far from his.

With both of our parents hospitalized, Sally and I were placed in foster care—a whirlwind of unfamiliar homes and unwelcoming faces.

My mother had been sick for as long as I could remember, long before my father's cancer diagnosis. Her illness was a constant presence in our lives, shaping the way we moved through each day. During those years, Sally and I often stayed at Eva's tiny home, where the closeness of the space brought a sense of comfort. But when my father fell ill, everything shifted. We were shuffled from Eva's house to Vivian's, our great-aunt, then sent to live with strangers for a day, a week, or longer. There was no permanence, no place to call home. We moved through so many houses, met so many people, that their names blurred together, lost in a haze of unfamiliar faces and borrowed rooms.

The worst of it was living under Vivian's roof. She was Eva's sister, but she never made us feel like family. Her bitterness surrounded me like a storm cloud, cold and unrelenting. I was a living reminder of her deceased son, a wound she refused to acknowledge. Her words cut deeper than any slap, her disdain heavy in every glance and every chore she assigned me. The house that should have been a refuge became a prison, and I learned that my tears were not welcome. There was no escape from her cruelty, no reprieve from her sharp tongue. We had nowhere else to go. Each day felt like a punishment.

The weight of those years pressed down on me, reshaping not just who I was but how I existed in the world. My shoulders curved inward under the burden of sorrow, my posture folding as if to make myself smaller, less visible. My gaze never lifted—I looked down, afraid to meet the eyes of those who might see too much. I moved through life as a shadow, silent and unseen, wishing I could disappear into the spaces between moments. The longing, the uncertainty, the grief—they became the language of my childhood, spoken in whispers and sobs, etched into the way I carried myself.

Before my father's illness, Sally and I often stayed with Vivian when my mother was hospitalized. At the time, I didn't understand her behavior, but as I grew older, I saw the battles she fought. Her struggles with alcoholism and severe obesity shaped her view of the world, and she saw Sally and me not as children in need but as a financial burden. She resented caring for us, despite the fact that before his illness, my father had helped with repairs and maintenance around her home in exchange for our stay.

Vivian's temper was unpredictable, her anger flaring over the smallest things. If we spilled something at dinner, we were forced to eat the ruined meal while her own family received fresh servings. The house smelled of beer, the scent of her drinking woven into every piece of furniture, every breath we took.

Her rules were strict, and her patience was thin. Any small noise set her off.

"You have to be quiet so I can relax," she snapped one afternoon, settling into her recliner with a heavy sigh.

Sally and I exchanged a glance but said nothing. We had learned that speaking made things worse.

Later, as we scrubbed our clothes by hand in the garage sink, Vivian hovered nearby, arms crossed.

"You two are lazy and spoiled," she huffed. "Back in my day, we didn't have machines to do everything for us."

I bit my tongue and focused on wringing out my shirt, pushing down the frustration that boiled inside me.

In the afternoons, we sat on the floor of the family room, afraid to move.

If I shifted to get comfortable, Vivian's glare pinned me in place.

"Don't talk while I'm watching my programs," she ordered, her eyes never leaving the screen.

Sally and I shrank into ourselves, trapped in a house where silence was the way to survive. To us, Vivian was a wicked witch, casting her misery like a spell we had no choice but to endure.

The time I spent in foster homes was no better. Grief, abandonment, and uncertainty clung to me like a second skin. My sleep-crying became a physical manifestation of everything I held inside, the emotions too overwhelming to contain during the day. The distress made it impossible to focus at school; my mind was too tangled in thoughts of my parents, of where I would sleep next, of how to survive another day.

Other children avoided me, their sneers and whispers cutting deeper than words spoken aloud. My tears made them uncomfortable, and they turned away with expressions of disgust. The adults were no different. My crying wore on their patience, their frustration surfacing in sharp words and cold silences.

Among my mother's relatives, some provided shelter and food, but their generosity was laced with resentment. To them, I was ungrateful, a burden they had no choice but to bear. Vivian was the harshest.

"Stop that crying," she snapped. "You're weak, and no one wants to deal with a sniveling child."

Her words stung, but I learned that showing my pain made things worse.

Kevin, Eva's son, was just two years older than me, but he relished every opportunity to make me feel smaller. He mocked my sobs, exaggerating them until he was doubled over in laughter. No matter how hard I tried to be obedient, to disappear into the background, my grief was unwelcome. The more I stayed silent, the more alone I felt.

At school, Fridays were filled with excitement—weekend plans, family outings, and laughter echoing through the halls. But for me, Fridays had lost their joy. My father was in the hospital, and there were no special lunches, no time together like before. I used to love Fridays, when Dad had a day off and would surprise Sally and me with a meal at home or take us out somewhere just for the fun of it. Those simple, happy moments had once made me feel safe. But now, Fridays were just another reminder of everything I had lost.

Our beloved seafood stand was special because it served the freshest, most delicious seafood straight from the Gulf of Mexico. Every visit meant shrimp caught that very morning, fried to perfection, and paired with golden, hand-cut french fries. The simplicity and quality of the food made it unforgettable, but what set it apart was the experience it created.

Sally and I loved eating with our fingers, savoring every bite as we laughed and soaked in the moment. It was more than just a meal—it was a cherished tradition, made even better by Dad's ritual of taking us to the boat docking areas along the shore. There, the salty breeze carried the cries of seagulls and the scent of the ocean. Feeding the gulls pieces of bread completed the day, turning a simple lunch into a treasured memory.

Every Friday at noon, my mind drifts back to those afternoons with my dad—the ones filled with the scent of salt in the air, the rhythmic rocking of boats, and the laughter of seagulls swooping overhead.

Lunchtime was more than a meal; it was an adventure. We'd sit by the water, watching as elegant sailboats and towering cargo ships passed through the harbor. The breeze carried the tang of the sea, tousling my red hair as I stood on tiptoe, eager to take it all in. My dad, steady and strong beside me, seemed to drink in the moment too.

Walking along the docks, we'd chat with fishermen and boat owners. I sometimes wondered if he ever wished for a son—someone to talk about fishing or sports with—but if he did, he never let it show. Instead, he held my hand, listened to my endless questions, and smiled with pride at his little redheaded daughter.

The seagulls were my favorite part. They soared overhead, their sharp cries beckoning me to toss bits of bread into the air. Mesmerized by their graceful dives and daring swoops, I'd inch closer to the edge of the water, lost in the spectacle. But before I could drift too far, my dad's steady hand would land on my shoulder, pulling me back with a gentle but firm grip. His chuckle—warm and knowing—wrapped around me like a safety net, a quiet reassurance that he was always there.

Those afternoons weren't just moments in time; they were *our* moments. And now, every Friday at noon, I find myself back there—standing by the water, my father's presence lingering in the breeze, the call of the seagulls still echoing in my heart.

During my time in foster homes, my routine revolved around school. After classes, I would head to the parking lot, hoping someone would arrive to take Sally and me home. We often waited for hours before someone showed up. It seemed like there was some coordination behind the scenes about where we would stay each day, involving my dad's friends at the telephone company.

During winter evenings, darkness would set in as we waited in the parking lot, leaving me hungry, thirsty, and overwhelmed by sadness and loneliness. All the other kids had gone home with their parents, the teachers had left, and still, we waited—unsure if anyone would come for us.

The most difficult place to stay was with my mother's side of the family. They had little patience for my tears and made it clear that I was an unwanted burden. Even their children questioned why I had to stay with them.

"Why do you have to live here?" one relative asked, her voice filled with confusion.

"Yeah, why can't you just go somewhere else?" another chimed in, staring at me with wide, expectant eyes.

I had no answer. How could I explain what I did not understand myself? That my father was sick? That there was nowhere else for me to go? That the very idea of *home* had become fragile and uncertain? Instead, I just shrugged, staring at the blanket and pillow on the floor—my makeshift bed.

Their questions weren't cruel, just honest. But honesty could still cut deep. Their parents' impatience hung heavy in every sigh, every sharp glance when I cried.

At night, the unfamiliar darkness swallowed me whole. I clutched my blanket tighter, pretending I was camping, even though I had never been on a real camping trip. My heart pounded at the thought of waking up in the middle of the night, needing to find the bathroom in a house that wasn't mine.

I squeezed my eyes shut and whispered the same silent prayer. Please don't let me get sick. Please let Dad get better. Please let this all be a nightmare I can wake up from.

Words like *foster care* and *homelessness* floated around me like shadows, but I refused to let them in. If I didn't say them, if I didn't acknowledge them, maybe they wouldn't be real. Maybe—just maybe—this wasn't my life after all.

In most of these homes, I was reminded not to touch anything and made to feel like an outsider. I suspect the other children resented me, afraid their parents might give me attention that should have been theirs.

During this time of profound sadness, my solace came from Mrs. Marion Horowitz. She and her husband, Nathan, were my dad's friends. Though older than my parents, they shared a deep bond. My mother disapproved of them because of their Jewish faith. She harbored prejudices, blaming Jews for Christ's death. Despite identifying as Catholic, she didn't practice her faith, but she clung to this belief.

The Horowitz family, however, showed me nothing but kindness. Marion and Nathan had four children, three boys and a girl, who welcomed me. Their home was a refuge for me.

Nathan, a CPA with his own accounting firm, and Marion, a Cornell graduate with a degree in horticulture, cultivated a home filled with love, care, and respect. Their spacious residence, nestled in an affluent neighborhood, stood in stark contrast to my family's modest house. Sunlight streamed through large windows, illuminating a beautifully landscaped backyard, while the cool hum of central air conditioning provided a welcome escape from the oppressive heat.

Yet, I never envied their wealth. I took pride in the home my father had provided for my mother, Sally, and me. Had cancer not taken hold of him, the house on the marina he had planned to buy would have given us the same kind of lifestyle. Still, the Horowitz's home offered me something invaluable—a temporary refuge from the disappointment and sadness that lingered in me.

Marion's kindness extended beyond words. She once rallied her synagogue friends to collect used clothes for me, tailored by a local Japanese seamstress. She treated me like one of her own, taking me to their country club to swim and play tennis or teaching me life skills like sewing and cooking.

One afternoon, Marion and I stood side by side in the kitchen, ready to take on the challenge of making an angel food cake from scratch.

"Alright, Cindy," she said with a smile, handing me the eggs. "Separate the yolks from the whites. No yolks, or the batter won't rise."

I nodded, eager to prove myself. I cracked the first egg, passing the yolk between the shells. One down. Then several more. We used an electric mixer to beat the whites until they formed fluffy peaks. But disaster struck when I added the yolks that I had spent so much time separating from the whites. My stomach clenched.

Marion gasped, then burst into laughter. "Oh no, sweetheart! The poor cake never even had a chance!"

I stared at the ruined mixture, my face burning with embarrassment. "I—I didn't mean to! I thought I was doing everything right."

She gave my shoulder a reassuring squeeze. "Of course you were. But hey, even the best bakers make mistakes. We'll just get more eggs!"

Relief flooded through me. No scolding, no harsh words—just warmth, understanding, and a twinkle in her eye.

"Let's go to the store," she said. "We'll get more eggs, and you can try again. I have faith in you."

If I had been in my mother's relatives' kitchen, I would have been met with sharp tongues and stern glares. But with Marion, mistakes weren't something to fear. They were part of learning—something to laugh about, fix, and move past with grace.

Later, when we pulled the cake from the oven—light, airy, and golden—I beamed with pride.

To this day, whenever I taste angel food cake, I don't just remember its sweetness. I remember Marion's laughter, her kindness, and the lesson she taught me: Mistakes were never the end of the world.

Back at my maternal grandmother Eva's house, life was a stark contrast. Eva's struggles with alcoholism often overshadowed any maternal instincts. One evening, she slumped in her chair, sighing.

"I could use a drink," she muttered. "But I ain't got no money."

I didn't respond, but something in her tone made my stomach twist. Later that night, I reached into a box where I had tucked away the money Marion had given me—the money meant for my college fund. My fingers grasped at nothing but air. The three dollars were gone.

Panic clawed at my chest as I searched through the small pile of clothes I owned. The money was nowhere. My throat tightened as I turned to Eva, who was watching me with an unreadable expression.

"Grandma," my voice cracked, but I forced the words out. "Do you know where my money is? The money Marion gave me for college. It's missing."

Her lips pursed, and for a brief moment, something flickered in her eyes—guilt? Annoyance? "Now why would I know anything about that?" she said, her voice too casual.

"Please," I whispered. "It was all I had. I need it."

She let out a sharp breath, shaking her head. "Maybe you lost it."

I swallowed hard, feeling the sting behind my eyes. I wanted to believe her. I wanted to believe this was just some mistake, that my own grandmother wouldn't steal from me. But deep down, I knew.

Though I told myself I forgave her, trust never returned.

Following this incident, I began to question things I had accepted without much thought. Why had her brothers and sisters completed high school, but Eva had not? Why did they speak English fluently while she struggled and spoke Czech? Why did they live in nice homes, while Eva barely got by? And why did they rarely visit or include her in their lives? The pieces didn't quite fit, and for the first time, I began to sense there were unspoken stories behind her isolation—stories that not only shaped who she was but also seemed to create distance between her siblings and both Sally and me.

My mother and Eva enabled each other's destructive habits—my mother's prescription drug addiction and Eva's alcoholism—further fracturing our family during my dad's illness. Instead of pulling together, we splintered apart. My dad had been the emotional and financial glue holding us together, and his illness left a void no one could fill.

Months before my father passed, Nanny made a rare visit to Eva's house. The tension between them was palpable, their silence heavy with old wounds and unspoken words. When Nanny arrived, she stood on the small porch, her eyes filled with quiet determination. She clung to the belief that my father would recover, but the others dismissed her optimism as crazy.

I didn't. I understood. Even as I held on to the hard truth my father had shared with me, I saw myself in her hope, in her refusal to let go.

"Nanny, I want to live at your house," I pleaded, my voice above a whisper.

She sighed, smoothing the fabric of her worn dress with steady hands. "You have to stay with Eva," she said. "Her house is close to your school."

"But I don't care about that," I protested, my throat tightening. "I just want to be with you."

I wanted her to say yes, to take Sally and me away from the suffocating walls of Eva's house. But she didn't.

When she turned to leave, my heart fractured. I knew she must have been troubled by the way we were living, yet she walked away, and I couldn't bring myself to call after her. Her presence, however brief, reminded me that love still existed in the cracks of our broken family. But her words didn't strengthen me. They diminished me. They made me feel small. Forgotten and unloved.

And as Nanny's car disappeared down the road, I stood there, silent, watching the last piece of comfort I had slip away.

Through it all, Marion and her family gave me glimpses of what a stable, loving home could be. Her gestures—a homemade storage box embroidered with my name, the special outings, and her quiet support—helped me hold on to hope. These moments of kindness sustained me during an otherwise dark time, planting the seed of resilience that would carry me through the years to come.

On several occasions, my father's employer organized food collections and delivered boxes of food to Eva's home—a small, aging house that lacked both air conditioning in the sweltering summers and a functioning heater in the winters. After separating from her husband, my grandmother struggled to make ends meet, stretching every dollar to provide for her two youngest children and for Sally and me.

The donated food was a blessing, filling empty cupboards with cans of soup, boxes of pasta, and bags of rice that would sustain us for several days. Yet, as grateful as I was for the kindness of strangers, I couldn't ignore the blunt reality it represented. The sight of those boxes—stacked in the dimly lit kitchen—was a reminder of how little we had, how much we relied on the goodwill of others just to eat. I felt the warmth of generosity, but also the embarrassment, knowing that without charity, hunger would have been another struggle.

When I was in third grade, two well-dressed women arrived at my classroom door after lunch. After a brief conversation with my teacher, they called for Sally and me. Following strangers felt risky, but their presence seemed connected to my survival, so I followed them.

As we sat in the back seat of their car, I gazed out the window, wishing we were on our way to the hospital to see my dad instead. I had no choice but to rely on my growing inner sense of awareness. The uncertainty of our destination unsettled me, but I felt powerless to change it.

We arrived at a prestigious department store—an elegant, three-story building that stood out as the first downtown store to feature both an elevator and air conditioning. At the time, it rivaled the sophistication of the shops on Fifth Avenue in New York City. Still, I couldn't quite understand why we were there.

The women gently guided us inside, asking if we'd like to try on some new clothes. Their kindness was unexpected and disarming. I found myself nodding in agreement—for both Sally and me. Sally rarely spoke, so I naturally took the lead.

I chose a beautiful dress, along with new shoes and socks to replace my threadbare ones.

Once dressed in our new outfits, the women drove us to the telephone company, where my dad had worked before his illness. I was confused—why were we here when my dad was in the hospital? As they introduced Sally and me as Sam Goble's daughters, the employees greeted us, their smiles filled with sympathy. It was bittersweet to be in this place so connected to my father while missing him.

I later realized that the employees had pooled their money to provide new clothes for Sally and me. Their compassion touched me, and I remain grateful for their generosity. Yet, as much as I appreciated the material gifts, what I longed for was my dad's presence. His love and guidance were irreplaceable, and his absence left a void nothing else could fill.

During my dad's illness, I was allowed to visit him at the hospital only three times. In the early stages, we met in the serene hospital atrium, a space filled with lush plants and the gentle sound of birds. The natural light and peaceful environment gave me a fleeting sense of comfort. At some point during my dad's stay in the hospital, health concerns about the birds led to the atrium's closure. Another place of solace disappeared.

Later, when my dad was transferred to a cancer center in Houston, I was permitted one brief visit. It was overwhelming. But those moments remain etched in my memory—a testament to his love.

That visit was the last time I saw my dad alive. Despite the hardships, I cherish the lessons he taught me and the strength he instilled in me. His love has carried me through the darkest times of my life, reminding me of the resilience he saw in me even when I couldn't see it myself.

The telephone company tried to have my dad admitted to a national cancer center in Los Angeles after his doctors in Houston had exhausted all options to help him. When that effort failed, they arranged for a private ambulance service to return him to the hospital in our hometown.

My years in foster care were a turbulent mix of heartbreak and unexpected kindness. Shuffled between homes, I was engulfed by rejection, shadowed by uncertainty, and haunted by the deep, persistent ache of my parents' absence. Yet, even in the darkest moments, glimmers of hope emerged—acts of compassion from strangers, fleeting moments of normalcy, and a strength I never knew I had.

Chapter 4

Loss That Lingers

∞

ON THE EVENING OF JULY 14, 1963, life felt fragile. My mother, Sally, my grandmother, Eva, and I were together again beneath the roof of my childhood home. Yet, my father's absence cast a heavy shadow over us. He had been transported back to the local hospital where his initial treatment had begun, while my youngest sister, Paulie, was elsewhere, her absence adding to the unspoken void. That night, my mother returned to the hospital to be with my father. I went to bed and had a dream so vivid it felt like an omen—a premonition sent to prepare me for the devastating news that awaited.

In the dream, I saw my father walking down the narrow hallway of our home. He stopped at the doorway of my bedroom, where I was sleeping beside Sally. He looked at me with an expression that conveyed a message beyond words: he had died. When I woke up the next morning, the dream replayed itself in real life. My mother entered my room and, in a quiet, almost hesitant voice, broke the news: "Your dad has died."

My dad had passed away during the night. I sat upright in bed, processing her words, already braced by the message I had received in my dream.

Beside me, Sally lay in her twin bed. When she woke and heard the news, she dissolved into sobs, her cries filled with raw, unfiltered anguish. Her pain was immediate, all-consuming. I, however, felt an eerie calm settle over me— an instinctive pull to console my sister and support my mother in whatever way I could.

Looking back, I now see that Sally's collapse was not just grief; it was the breaking point of a long, silent struggle with her mental health. My mother had never spoken of our father's terminal illness—nor of the psychiatric battles she and Sally would later face. Her silence left us to navigate our pain alone, deepening the wounds we were already carrying.

I kept my dream a secret for decades, sharing it with no one until I reached my thirties. It was a personal bond between my father and me—a spiritual gift that gave me the strength to face his loss with grace. Even now, I feel his presence, and in life's challenging moments, I draw on the love he poured into me as a child.

My father's death on Monday, July 15, 1963, was nothing short of a whirlwind of sorrow and confusion. My mother, exhausted and emotional from being at my father's side as he took his last breath, retreated back home to her bedroom under the pretense of resting. But resting was not her goal. She swallowed a dangerous cocktail of prescription medications. Her disoriented, stumbling state alerted Eva, who called her sister, Vivian, to drive my mother to the emergency room. My mother's absence at my father's funeral added to the ache of her physical and emotional distance from me. It would be weeks before I saw her again.

During the funeral preparations, our home became a hub of mourning, with relatives and friends flooding in, bringing casseroles and condolences. But I felt out of place. While others found solace in shared memories and the constant hum of conversation, I was overwhelmed. The noise, the movement, the well-meaning gestures—all of it seemed to deepen my sense of disconnection. I was grieving in a quieter way, one that didn't fit the rhythm of the house. Marion offered me refuge at her home once again. Her kindness was a sustenance amid the overwhelming sadness, a calm and steady space where I could begin to breathe again.

The next afternoon, my mother's sister, Margot, and her husband, Bobby, took Sally and me to the funeral home. It was my first time entering such a place, and the sight of my father in an open casket shocked me. My chest tightened, and I wanted nothing more than to run, to wake up from this nightmare.

Then, the unthinkable happened. Relatives encouraged me to approach his coffin and pose for photographs beside it. The idea felt cruel and incomprehensible. Did they think I might forget this moment, that I would need proof of my father's death to cement the pain in my memory? The suggestion sent a chill through me. My father had always been proud, private—he would never have wanted to be photographed in death. I was sure of that. Yet, here they were, treating this moment as if it needed to be documented, as if grief should be captured and preserved like a family portrait.

I felt sick. This was not a happy occasion, not something I would ever want to look back on. But I was a child, and I was taught to obey. So I swallowed my revulsion, my grief, my desperate wish to disappear, and I stood where they told me to stand. I suppressed my own sorrow for the sake of those around me, unsure if anyone even considered how I felt.

The wake unraveled into a dramatic spectacle. Sally's cries swelled into piercing screams, Nanny sobbed and was uncontrollable, and in the midst of the chaos, my Aunt Dorothy collapsed in a faint. Surrounded by the turmoil, I stood apart, watching the adults with a deepening sense of disbelief. At just ten years old, childhood had slipped away—I had been forced to grow up overnight.

Marion rescued me again the following day, taking me back to her home so I could avoid the three-day vigils at the funeral home. I confided in her, expressing my deep discomfort and refusal to return. Her understanding and advocacy allowed me a reprieve from the relentless sadness that permeated every moment.

As we sat at her kitchen table, the scent of dinner filling the air, I hesitated before speaking. Marion waited with patience, her kind eyes encouraging me to say what I needed to.

"I can't go back," I admitted, in a whisper. "I can't stand another minute in that place, watching people cry, hearing the same condolences over and over. It feels… suffocating."

Marion nodded, setting her glass of iced tea down. "I understand, Cindy. Funerals can be overwhelming."

I looked down at my hands, picking at my fingernails. "I don't want to keep reliving it. I just… I don't want to go back."

She reached across the table, giving my hand a reassuring squeeze. "Then you won't. I'll ask your relatives if you can stay a few extra days here."

A lump formed in my throat at the relief washing over me. "But won't they be upset?"

She smiled. "People grieve in different ways. Yours doesn't have to look like theirs. I'll talk to them."

Tears pricked my eyes, but this time, they weren't from sadness. "Thank you, Marion. I don't know what I'd do without you."

"You don't have to," she said. "Let me take care of this for you."

On Friday morning, I attended my father's funeral service at a Catholic church. Members of the orchid guild, with whom Nanny and her second husband were longtime members, adorned the casket with a beautiful orchid arrangement. Despite the church's grandeur and the solemnity of the ceremony, there was one glaring absence: my mother.

At the gravesite, the US Navy rendered full military honors for my father, a ceremony that was both moving and terrifying. My father's casket was now draped with the American flag. The slow, mournful notes of "Taps" cut through the silence like a blade, each one echoing the finality of his death in a way nothing else had. The crisp, precise folding of the flag felt like a countdown to the moment he would be lowered into the ground, an irreversible step toward a reality I wasn't ready to accept. And then, the gun salute—sharp, sudden, and unrelenting—startled me to my core, each shot a jarring reminder of the void his absence had created.

I stood there, feeling small and unmoored, proud of my father yet overwhelmed by a profound loneliness. That flag, a symbol of his sacrifice, should have been placed into my mother's hands. Instead, it was given to Sally, who was so distraught that accepting it was almost impossible. The moment felt incomplete, as if something essential had been lost in my mother's absence. Amid the structure of military tradition, I felt the weight of everything that had been broken, the unbearable wrongness of a farewell that didn't feel whole.

As we left the cemetery, relatives pointed out the long line of cars in the funeral procession, a testament to the many lives my father had touched. But amid the crowd, I noticed my father's side of the family standing at a distance behind those gathered at the gravesite, their presence almost hidden. It wasn't until later that I understood why—they had stayed back because it was a Catholic burial service, and they were Protestant.

The division between my parents' families had always been there, unspoken yet undeniable. My mother's side never liked my father's side, and the feeling was mutual. I had spent my life caught in the middle, trying to please both but never succeeding. That day, their physical distance mirrored the emotional chasm that had always existed, and I couldn't help but feel stranded between them. I longed for the comfort of family, yet there was no unity to be found— the silent weight of old resentments that had outlived even my father.

In the days and weeks that followed, the reality of my father's absence settled over me like a heavy blanket. Not long after my father's funeral, the family sorted through his personal possessions. Still heartbroken, I found it even more painful to watch as some family members laid claim to specific items, viewing them for their monetary worth rather than their sentimental significance. Some items could not be shared to multiple people, like my dad's vintage car. My mother's youngest sister, Aunt Audrey, asked for the car so she could commute to her administrative job. She sounded entitled to the car, citing the help she had given my parents during their illnesses. The car was a repayment of debt she felt owed.

Sally, who cherished my father, found sentimental meaning in his stereo, watch, and some clothing items. She insisted on having them as keepsakes. On the other hand, Nanny requested his photos and camera equipment, but my mother wished to keep them. There were numerous black-and-white photos, color photos, slides, and family films that my mother stored in an outdoor unlocked closet.

Tragedy struck when some underage boys caused a fire while smoking cigarettes near the closet. All the photographs taken by my dad were lost in the heartbreaking incident. I didn't care as much for my father's material things, but the loss of the photos—his images, memories caught on film, a history of my family—were now gone.

It seemed like everyone in the family wanted something that had once belonged to my dad. The situation led to arguments, tears, and bitter words as relatives vied for specific objects. Memories of him were the most precious things I held within my heart, and I knew that no matter where life took me, those memories would remain.

Every morning after my dad's funeral and before I got out of bed, I would ask myself the same questions: "Why did I wake up? Why am I here? What is my purpose?" It was hard for me to fall asleep at night, and I never wanted to be alone in the dark. My father had been asleep when a clot formed in his leg and killed him. I thought that I could also die as I slept, but I also knew that I wanted to be with my dad wherever he was.

Weeks after my dad's death, near Labor Day, my mother and her relatives took us to the seashore. On a remote stretch of beach, we collected seashells and played in the water. Then I went into the water with Aunt Margot and Uncle Bobby. Margot used a small Styrofoam board to float, but the waves kept pulling it from her hands, and I helped retrieve it. Bobby returned to the shore, waving off our calls for him to rejoin us.

As Margot and I played, a strong undercurrent began pulling us further from shore. Margot screamed for Bobby, but he couldn't hear her and assumed we were having fun. The waves separated us, and although Margot swam back to find me, I didn't know how to swim and was too weak to fight the waves. Exhausted and terrified, I clung to the Styrofoam board when I could, but the waves kept wrenching it from my hands.

Margot told me to say the Catholic Act of Contrition, but I cried out, "Please, God, please help me." I had heard these same words before—when my father was in agony, suffering in pain during his illness. It was a miracle that Bobby noticed how far we had drifted and swam out to rescue us. Grabbing both Margot and me, he helped us reach the shore.

When I stood on the sand, I cried, overwhelmed by the realization that I had chosen to live. That moment shook me to my core, leaving me with a question I had never before dared to ask: Why did I want to live? Until then, my existence had felt dictated by others—by the demands and neglect of those around me, by the expectations placed upon me, by a sense of duty to endure rather than a will to thrive. But in the vastness of the ocean, in the terrifying possibility of being swallowed by it, I was faced with a choice. And I chose life.

This experience became a catalyst for my awakening, a moment that shattered the passivity of my survival and awakened in me an undeniable truth: I was meant for more. My father's words echoed in my mind, reminding me to care for myself. I saw with painful clarity that my mother and relatives could not provide the care I needed. There was no life jacket, no lifeguard, no protection from the harshness of the sun on my sensitive skin. If I wanted to be safe, if I wanted to live, I had to take responsibility for my own well-being.

But this realization went beyond physical safety; it planted the first seeds of self-worth. I began to understand that my life had meaning beyond what others dictated. The near-drowning forced me to look inward, to seek solace not in the external world, which had so often failed me, but in a deeper, unseen presence that had answered my desperate plea for help. That moment of surrender in the water, when I called out to God, was the first time I felt my connection to something greater than myself. I had always believed in God, but now, I experienced the Divine in a way that was personal and real.

From that day forward, my life shifted. I no longer endured—I sought. I explored what it meant to nourish my body, my mind, and my soul. Self-care became more than a necessity; it became an act of love, a declaration that I was worth protecting. I began paying attention to the things that fed my spirit, from the books I read to the quiet moments of reflection where I could hear my own voice, unfiltered and true.

In time, I realized that my search for meaning was not about finding a singular answer but about embracing the journey itself. Every experience, every challenge, and every moment of grace was a step toward understanding who I was meant to be. Looking back, I see that day in the ocean not as a moment of fear but as a sacred turning point. It was the moment I first felt a deep connection to my Source, a knowing that I was guided, protected, and meant to live with purpose. And from that moment on, I would never again be content to survive—I would seek, I would grow, and I would live with intention.

My mother's drug abuse and neglect shaped every corner of my childhood. While Sally's medical needs and Paulie's role as the youngest demanded much of her attention, I often felt invisible—a shadow in my own home. Even when she was present, her emotional absence left a void I struggled to fill.

One night, when I was five or six, I helped her wash dishes, chatting as I dried plates. I shared my dreams, hoping for a flicker of interest. When I said, "Mommy, I love you," her silence cut deep, a hollow absence of warmth. This scene played out countless times, her indifference an ever-present shadow. My efforts to earn her approval—a paint-by-number picture I created for her before starting first grade—were met with the same cold indifference. Her lack of acknowledgment crushed my budding confidence as an artist.

In the sixth grade, I won first place in the local science fair—a blue-ribbon project that had taken weeks of work. My teacher beamed with pride, my classmates congratulated me, but when I brought the ribbon home, eager for even the smallest nod of approval, my mother gave a moment's notice. No praise, no interest—another achievement swallowed by her indifference.

Later, I came to understand that my mother battled undiagnosed mental illness, buried traumas, and an addiction to prescription drugs. This knowledge didn't excuse her neglect, but it offered context. Stigma surrounding mental health kept these struggles unspoken, leaving our family without resolution. Mounting medical bills from her frequent doctor visits added financial strain.

Often, I wondered how different life might have been if my father had lived—if his steady, protective love might have shielded us from chaos and allowed my dreams to flourish. I imagined a childhood where warmth and encouragement replaced cold indifference, where my small victories—like a painted picture or a whispered "I love you"—were met with pride instead of silence. In those daydreams, I was not a child trying to prove my worth but one who belonged, secure in the presence of a father who saw and cherished me.

I envisioned a home filled with laughter, not the quiet strain of unspoken sorrow. My father's guidance might have steered me toward my dreams—working as an engineer at the telephone company where he had worked. I pictured us living in a big, new marina home, the kind with wide windows that let in the golden glow of the evening sun. A boat bobbing at the dock, waiting for family outings where joy wasn't something to chase but something natural, effortless. In this life, our home was a gathering place, alive with friends and relatives, their voices weaving together in harmony, not weighed down by the tension of my mother's struggles.

But those were dreams—ones I clung to when the silence in our home grew too heavy. My father's absence left a void too vast to fill, and reality pressed in with its unyielding truths. Instead of encouragement, I learned resilience. Instead of security, I learned how to navigate uncertainty. And instead of the steady love I longed for, I learned to find strength within myself.

Despite her rejection, small moments of hope kept my determination alive. One morning, as I stood by the driveway to go to school, I envisioned a brighter future—a life filled with love, happiness, and even a bloodhound like the one I had admired before my father fell ill. When my mother dismissed my dreams, I refused to let them go. "One day," I declared, "I'm going to live in California and have a wonderful job in Beverly Hills."

Looking back, it's remarkable to realize that I did just that. Though my journey wasn't without struggle, the lessons I learned in childhood became the foundation for my personal successes. In a twist of fate, I fulfilled my dream of living in Los Angeles and working in Beverly Hills. When I later relocated to the East Coast for a position in New York City, my life was unexpectedly enriched—not by one but by six beloved bloodhounds.

In fourth grade, at just nine years old, I experienced a revelation that would alter the course of my life forever. It was the moment I realized I didn't need my mother's approval to thrive. Up until that point, I had clung to the hope that if I could be good enough, smart enough, or lovable enough, she would accept me. But that acceptance never came. The rejection, as devastating as it was, carried an unexpected gift: clarity. I saw, perhaps for the first time, that my worth was not defined by her love—or lack thereof.

At an age when most children are still nestled in the comfort of parental guidance, I stood at a crossroads between despair and determination. I chose determination. I began to see my future not as an extension of my pain but as something I could shape with my own hands. I closed my eyes and envisioned the milestones that would one day define my success: high school graduation, a college degree, a stable career, and a home where I felt safe and secure. These weren't just dreams; they became my guiding stars, illuminating the path ahead.

I made a vow to myself that no challenge would break me. Every obstacle would be met with resilience, every setback a lesson rather than a defeat. I promised that one day, I would no longer be the child yearning for approval—I would be the person who had risen above the circumstances that sought to define me. My mother's rejection no longer felt like an insurmountable loss; instead, it became the catalyst for my drive to succeed.

Even at nine years old, I understood that the road ahead would not be easy. I knew loneliness would accompany me at times, that fear and doubt would whisper in the shadows. But I also knew something more profound: I had the power to rise. I had the power to create a life built not on the wounds of the past but on the limitless possibilities of the future.

This was my turning point. This was the moment I became more than just a child searching for love—I became the architect of my own destiny.

While my life was filled with excessive stress and worry, Sally faced continuous challenges with her mental health. Her struggles were further compounded by a tragic accident, making her journey even more difficult.

One summer, just before she started first grade, Sally climbed onto the railing of our back porch, pretending to be a circus performer. It was forbidden by our parents, but she didn't understand the danger. She lost her balance and fell headfirst onto the cement driveway below. I found her unconscious, ran to alert my mother, and watched as panic erupted. At the hospital, her head was bandaged, and she lay unresponsive. At first, she couldn't see, and my parents feared the worst. Though they hoped her vision would return, the days of uncertainty felt endless. Then the darkness lifted, and she could see again. But the accident left her forever changed, amplifying her existing disabilities.

Sedatives kept Sally asleep for much of the day, deepening her isolation. At school, she was neglected by teachers and tormented by classmates. Some even questioned why I was so smart when she was not. Though she was older, by the time I was four, I had already surpassed her on an emotional and intellectual level—a shift that complicated our sibling bond. Despite being urged to distance myself from her, I remained by her side during recess, unwilling to abandon her.

During our father's illness, I longed for Sally's comfort, but she couldn't grasp the gravity of what was happening. Yet, her occasional willingness to hold my hand in the dark of night when we were living in foster care homes offered a rare and bittersweet solace.

Later in life, Sally became a mother. After enduring two miscarriages, she gave birth to a son. The father's identity remained a mystery, reflecting the unspoken secrets that surrounded our family. Through it all, Sally taught me about generosity, unconditional love, and the importance of standing by those who need support.

Her presence shaped my life in ways I continue to carry with me. Growing up alongside her struggles made me grateful for both my physical and mental health. It instilled in me a deep compassion for those with mental illness and disabilities, shaping how I see and support others. Sally's life, though often marked by hardship, left an enduring impact on my journey, reminding me of the power of empathy, love, and kindness.

Paulie was five years my junior—a gentle child with fair skin, piercing blue eyes, and long, ever-changing hair that danced between blonde and brunette. As a baby, Paulie was full of promise, but her life, like mine, was shaped by the heartbreak that fractured our family.

When our father was diagnosed with terminal cancer, Paulie was eighteen months old. While Sally and I were sent to foster care, Paulie stayed with Nanny. My memories of her as a baby are faint, but I recall how cherished she was before everything fell apart. The next time I saw Paulie was at our father's burial when she was five. She had grown so much that I did not recognize her—a painful reminder of the time and distance that separated us.

Months after losing my father in July 1963, the nation was plunged into mourning with the assassination of President John F. Kennedy that November. Watching his televised funeral stirred fresh grief within me, as I couldn't help but draw painful parallels. Little Caroline Kennedy and I had both lost our fathers, but the contrast was stark—while her loss was shared with an entire nation, mine felt isolating and personal.

Caroline and John Jr., close in age to Paulie and me, mourned their father with their mother, Jacqueline Kennedy, who was steadfast by their side. While the Kennedy children had the steady presence of their mother, my siblings and I faced our loss without such stability. Our mother, consumed by prescription drug dependency, was absent, leaving her mother to care for us during this fragile and painful time.

While Mrs. Kennedy embodied strength and grace, my mother's struggles left her hospitalized during my father's funeral. The differences were glaring. The Kennedys maintained their privileged lifestyle with ease, while my family was buried under medical debt, struggling to survive. Education, too, highlighted the disparity. Higher education was a given for the Kennedys, but for me, it was an uphill battle—made possible through Veterans Aid discovered in my senior year of high school.

These contrasts ignited a quiet resolve within me. Jacqueline Kennedy's strength inspired me to rise above my hardships, even as the weight of loss lingered in my heart. Despite the glaring disparities, I carried forward a determination to create a better future, one defined by resilience and hope.

Before my father's death, life felt whole, a patchwork of connection and kindness stitched together by shared experiences. Neighbors waved from across the street, and laughter often spilled from open windows. Belonging was a quiet comfort, woven into day-to-day life that I never noticed. It was the way things were—a world where love and community were constants.

But grief has a way of slipping in unnoticed, quiet and insidious. My father's passing marked the first tear in the fabric of our lives. What once felt secure began to fray. Family gatherings, once brimming with warmth and laughter, grew quieter. Visits became less frequent, replaced by excuses and strained silences. Bonds that had once seemed eternal loosened under the weight of sorrow, as if grief had sown seeds of distance between us.

Then came the waves of change—relocations, financial struggles, and family disputes, each pulling at the threads of what remained. Our once tight-knit community unraveled into distant, solitary lives. The streets where neighbors had once gathered became quiet and unfamiliar. Faces I had known since childhood turned away, preoccupied with their own burdens. I wondered if neighbors were fearful that cancer, like tuberculosis or polio, might be contagious. The neighborhood, once alive with shared joys, became little more than a collection of houses, their doors closed, their windows dark.

At home, the silence was even heavier. It filled the spaces where love and connection had once thrived, pressing in like an unwelcome guest. Conversations dwindled to curt exchanges, and the warmth of togetherness faded into memory.

The loss of community mirrored the unraveling of my own life. Each thread that loosened, each bond that broke, left me grieving—not just for the people I had lost but for the intangible sense of belonging that had slipped through my fingers. What remained was a fragmented existence marked by an ache for the connection that once defined me.

Yet, even in the midst of isolation, a quiet hope lingered. Memories of joy and togetherness glimmered, like distant stars in a dark sky. They whispered that life wasn't meant to be faced alone, that the fabric of connection could perhaps be rewoven.

The question that haunted me was whether those bonds could be rebuilt or if the unraveling had forever changed the shape of my life. Could I create something new from the scattered threads, or was I destined to carry the weight of that loss forever?

Part II
The Storm of Adolescence

Chapter 5

A New Reality with a Stepfather and Stepsiblings

AFTER MY FATHER'S passing, life fell further into deep chaos. Grief swallowed my mother whole, pulling her into a darkness she never escaped. She withdrew from the world, drowning herself in prescription drugs that numbed her pain but hollowed her out. The woman who had once been my mother became a ghost, erratic and unreachable.

The telephone company initially hired my mother as a secretary, but she was dismissed within weeks. Family friends tried to help by securing her another position at a geological firm, hoping she could regain stability. But she was either absent, lost in a drug-induced haze, or too emotionally unstable to manage her responsibilities. When she was terminated a few days later, no one was surprised. Her unreliability stood in sharp contrast to my father's steady, disciplined work ethic—a difference so striking it was impossible to ignore. Her dismissal was a setback, another fracture in the already crumbling foundation of our lives.

As the months passed, my mother's addiction deepened. I would wake up to find her wandering the house, lost in a stupor, or worse—collapsed on the floor. Each time, I wondered if this would be the night I wouldn't be able to wake her. One night, I found her in the kitchen. A few days earlier, she had stored a whole watermelon in the freezer, and now in her drugged state, she felt hungry and wanted to eat it. She stumbled into the kitchen, gripping a butcher knife in one hand as she reached into the freezer with the other. Her fingers slipped, the knife jerked, and blood spilled across the linoleum. The icy watermelon rolled away as she clutched her hand, dazed.

She fumbled for the phone and called her mother for help. But her mother had never driven a car, so she, in turn, called Vivian and her husband, pleading that they rush to take my mother to the emergency room. When they arrived, the situation was wrapped in reassurances and explanations. "An accident," they said. But I knew better. I had seen it too many times. My mother was more than clumsy. She was overdosing, lost in the numbing fog of her pills. And with each passing night, I feared she was slipping further away, beyond my reach. The illusion of control she tried to maintain was sliding more from her grasp, and with it, the safety of Sally, Paulie, and me.

In June 1966, as Sally and I were finishing eighth grade, we were stuck in an in-between space where nothing felt certain. The simple question of where we would go to school next was one more uncertainty in a life already overflowing with them. Each day felt like standing on shifting sands, bracing for the next upheaval.

A decision my mother made altered the trajectory of our lives. She married Doug Hoffmann, a widowed tax accountant and motel owner she had met while filing her income taxes. Their connection was forged in shared losses. Their whirlwind romance culminated in a simple church ceremony two months after they met.

My mother wore a pale blue two-piece outfit with a matching pillbox hat, an ensemble that exuded a polished grace—financed by Doug. Yet beneath the refined exterior, a stark reality loomed. There was no joyous reception and no celebratory gathering. The absence of festivity reflected the speed of their union and the somber undercurrents of unspoken truths that shaped it.

To me, the pillbox hat became more than an accessory. It was a symbol of my mother's constructed facade—a glossy exterior concealing the unruliness and pain of her struggles with addiction. Behind the careful poise and the neat seams of her outfit lay a life frayed by hardship, stitched together by fleeting moments of stability.

Sally, Paulie, and I met Doug's eight children for the first time at the wedding, a moment that felt nothing short of surreal. Ranging in age from ten years older than me to seven years younger, they were complete strangers— yet I was expected to call them family. I never had time to process their presence before my mother and Doug departed for a honeymoon in New York City, leaving us behind with no mention of when they would return. Her abrupt departure, without so much as a proper goodbye, left me with a hollow sense of abandonment.

While my mother and Doug were away, Paulie was separated from Sally and me. Paulie stayed with Aunt Audrey, while Sally and I were put on a bus to Nanny's house. It was our first solo trip—frightening and uncertain. We had no money and no way to contact Nanny by phone. Somehow, we navigated the trip and stayed safe.

When we arrived, Nanny greeted us at the door, her home a refuge despite her own struggles with rheumatoid arthritis and heart disease. I found comfort in the quiet routine of helping her with household chores and crossword puzzles, small moments of stability in an otherwise uncertain time. But as usual, she brought up our Catholic upbringing, a familiar strain in our conversations. When all we needed was love and acceptance, we were instead met with judgment—another reminder that true refuge was never quite within reach.

Our brief respite at Nanny's was shattered by a phone call from Aunt Audrey, insisting we return to her home for church. The demand angered Nanny, who saw it as an intrusion on her time with us. With little warning, we were sent back to Aunt Audrey's, where we were met with sharp lectures about Nanny's supposed shortcomings. Sally and I, accustomed to being caught in the middle of family disputes, bore the blame in silence, our longing for peace and permanency growing with each upheaval.

As my mother and Doug approached Houston, the illusion of a fresh start crumbled. She began feeling unwell, and Doug, concerned, admitted her to the same hospital where she had been hospitalized multiple times during my father's illness. There, the full extent of her addiction became undeniable, and mounting medical debts also came to light. Doug was blindsided. His children, already wary of my mother's intentions, saw her hospitalization as proof that she was a gold digger. Their resentment deepened as her dependence on prescription drugs became impossible to ignore.

After my mother's discharge, she and Doug abandoned their honeymoon plans and returned home. We then moved into Doug's motel. The busy, impersonal atmosphere offered little sense of home. First and foremost, it was a motel—a place of constant movement, filled with a steady stream of guests and endless noise. The transience of it all left me longing for a real home.

To my surprise, Doug's children welcomed me with warmth, despite the tension and division stirred by my mother, Sally, and Paulie. Adjusting to life as one of eleven siblings—five older, five younger—came naturally, as I remained a middle child both before and after the family merger.

Doug's children viewed my mother with suspicion, resenting her presence as an unwelcome stepmother. Sally, the most outspoken in her disapproval, refused to call Doug anything but "Mr. Hoffmann," her defiance a constant reminder of the fractures within our family. Paulie kept her distance from both Doug and his children, reinforcing the divide.

On the other side, Doug's oldest daughter, Jessica, and her sister Ashley formed their own private alliance, further isolating us from any sense of unity. Jessica was six months older than me, and Ashley was the same age as Paulie. Yet despite being surrounded by ten other children, I felt alone—caught in the middle of a family weighed down by resentment and disappointment.

Though we lived under one roof, we were not a family in any meaningful sense. Instead, we were two factions—each burdened by grief, resentment, and the disorientation of displacement. We maintained appearances, posing for family photos and playing the part of a cohesive unit. Behind closed doors, the emotional distance was palpable, and conflicts simmered just beneath the surface.

My mother's halfhearted attempts to bridge the divide often fell flat, leaving the household strained and fragmented. She sometimes prepared meals with Doug, standing beside him in the kitchen as if the act of cooking together might dissolve the tension between her and Doug's children. Yet, the silence between them was louder than any conversation they forced themselves to have. She made attempts to be social with Doug's relatives, smiling through stiff interactions and nodding along to stories in which she had no real investment. But these gestures, however well-intended, felt more like obligations than genuine efforts at connection. Whatever warmth she tried to manufacture never quite took hold, dissipating as soon as it appeared.

Amid the discord and to my surprise, I found an ally in Doug. While Sally and Paulie kept him at arm's length, I was drawn to his steady, gentle demeanor. He exuded a quiet strength that offered a rare sense of stability. I nicknamed him "Sugar Bear," inspired by the playful mascot of a popular cereal whose demeanor reminded me of him. Doug became a source of warmth and kindness.

Even with his best efforts to create solidity, Doug faced impossible challenges. An Ivy League graduate, army veteran, and an only child, he carried discipline and resilience into the pandemonium of our lives. Yet, my mother's addiction and extravagant spending drained him. His children resented her, Sally struggled in school, and Paulie remained distant. Doug bore the weight of responsibility alone, his quiet perseverance a testament to both his character and his suffering.

One afternoon, I pushed open the entrance door to the motel office, my arms aching from carrying books home from school. Doug sat behind the desk, papers spread before him, his brow furrowed in concentration. The room smelled of cigarette smoke and old paper.

"Where's Mom?" I asked, setting my books beside the chair.

Doug exhaled through his nose; eyes still fixed on the tax documents. "I had to take her back to the hospital to dry out again."

I gripped the back of the chair, my stomach tightening. "When will she be home?"

He looked up, his eyes tired. "I don't know. Could be weeks, maybe months."

I nodded. This had happened before. It would happen again.

Doug leaned back, rubbing a hand over his face. "Your mom needs more than just drying out. She needs to see a psychiatrist. She's got … mental problems."

I sank into the chair across from him. A wave of relief washed over me. At least I was here with Doug and not with Eva and her family. Or worse, with strangers. I knew where kids like me ended up when no one wanted them.

The office fell silent except for the scratch of Doug's pen as he returned to his tax filings. Tax season had begun, stretching until May. I watched him work, the numbers and calculations meaningless to me but his presence grounding.

After a few minutes, I found my voice. "Doug … if you and Mom get a divorce, could you adopt me?"

His pen hesitated for the briefest second before continuing. "It's too expensive to adopt a child."

I swallowed hard. "How much?"

"Several thousand dollars."

I forced a small nod, as if I understood. Maybe I did. Maybe it wasn't just about money. Maybe it would have looked strange, adopting me and not Sally and Paulie. Maybe no one wanted me—not even my own mother. And I no longer wanted her either.

I twisted my hands in my lap. What did it take to be loved? To be wanted?

Decades later, after years of therapy, I would come to understand that I had never known love. I had clung to the smallest gestures—thimble-sized affection—because I didn't know anything else. I felt certain of my father's love, a distant but precious memory from childhood. I held on to it as if it were a flickering flame in the darkness, even as the years stretched further away.

I had to learn to love myself. To accept that I was enough. But back then, I didn't know how. I had always been an overachiever, pushing myself beyond my limits, hoping that an A on a report card or a promotion at work would mean I was worthy. But no grade, no title, no achievement ever made me feel loved. It meant I had met expectations.

And even then, it never felt like enough.

Looking back, I see the impossible position Doug was in. At the time, his brief explanations felt like indifference. But now I recognize it as exhaustion. He was trying to hold together something that had already fractured beyond repair. He must have known it was a losing battle, yet he stayed, providing what structure he could in a household that resisted stability at every turn.

Though I never saw a happy marriage between him and my mother, I wonder now if he ever allowed himself to hope things might improve—or if he endured because that was what he had been taught to do. Perhaps, in his own quiet way, staying felt like the one safe option for himself, his eight children, and his three stepchildren. By then, he was already in his forties, and the prospect of a failed marriage—another upheaval—must have weighed on him. Divorce carried a stigma, and remarriage might not have been easy or even acceptable in social circles. But more than that, I think he saw the mistake he had made—how he and my mother had rushed into marriage, how blind he had been to the warning signs. Maybe by the time he realized it, he felt it was too late to undo.

Living in a motel was far from the adventure I might have imagined as a child. Doug's "house," carved out of a section of the motel, felt more like a temporary shelter than a home. It was cramped, with just enough room for the essentials—a small office with a half-bath, a narrow kitchen, a living room, a family room, and two tiny bedrooms with a shared full bath. At night, space was divided not by walls but by necessity. Sally, Paulie, and I slept in the living room, while Doug and my mother shared the family room. My stepsiblings were tucked into the two bedrooms, which, during peak travel season, doubled as extra motel rooms—further reinforcing the sense that our living space was never truly ours.

Though I wasn't living as a foster child at the time, the instability and lack of privacy echoed the conditions I had endured earlier. The backyard, which opened into the parking lot, served as a constant reminder of our impermanence. It was as though our lives had been reduced to the transience of the motel guests we lived among.

At first glance, the motel's in-ground pool seemed like a luxury. I thought it might offer a reprieve from the day-to-day grind. But the novelty wore off. Nights were fractured by the incessant chime of the office doorbell, jolting me awake each time a new guest arrived. I often found myself trudging through schooldays in a haze of exhaustion. After a year, the cramped living space in Doug's converted house became too much, and Sally and I were moved into Room 12—a bare-bones motel room that stripped life down to its most basic form.

The darker realities of life at the motel revealed themselves with the passage of time. Doug's business wasn't just about providing shelter—it catered to an ever-changing stream of guests, many carrying burdens too heavy to name. I came to understand, in ways no teenager should, the meaning behind room rentals by the hour. Women in precarious situations—some pregnant—became part of the motel's backdrop. Prostitutes were more than visitors; they were fixtures, their presence as constant as the hum of the flickering neon sign outside.

I always had a nagging feeling that something wasn't right. I sensed the unease in the air, the way certain guests avoided eye contact, the urgency in their movements. At the time, I didn't have the words to define it, but my instincts told me danger lurked beneath the surface of those transactions. Now, with my awareness of human trafficking, I can look back and see the motel for what it was—a place where people were used, discarded, and often trapped. The signs were all there, yet no one around me acknowledged them. Not Doug, not my mother, not any of our relatives. If they noticed, they didn't care. And if they cared, they did nothing.

They were woven into the very fabric of the motel—in the quiet shuffle of their footsteps across the cracked pavement and in the way their existence shaped the rhythm of day-to-day life. The bedsheets carried the scent of hurried encounters, the front desk bell rang in a steady cadence of silent transactions, and the walls, peeling from years of neglect, absorbed the secrets whispered within them. Housekeepers learned to avert their eyes, to sweep away the remnants of lives unraveling behind locked doors. Even the air felt weighed with their stories—whispers of desperation, survival, and resignation that lingered long after they had gone.

Then, one day, a housekeeper found a dead body in the closet of one of the rooms. She quit on the spot, her silent departure leaving behind a chilling void—a reminder that some ghosts never checked out.

My mother, consumed by her own needs and dulled by the influence of prescription drugs, never considered the well-being of those around her. Doug, on the other hand, did not see us as children. We were workers, expected to contribute to the motel's upkeep rather than indulge in childhood. There was no room for immaturity—we were reminded not to act like babies.

When the housekeeper didn't show up, Doug enlisted his younger sons—Don, Jeff, and Dennis—to clean, and sometimes Jessica, Ashley, and I joined them. Stripping stained sheets, scrubbing grimy toilets, and picking up the remnants of guests' lives left behind became part of our routine. Each room told its own story, a silent testament to the desperate, transient lives that passed through. Some were vandalized; others contained forgotten traces of their occupants—syringes, empty pill bottles, and condoms.

I didn't know what condoms were or what they were used for, but Jessica did. She explained in matter-of-fact words that they prevented pregnancy. She also informed me, with the certainty of a childhood misconception, that tampons were only for married women—something I refused to believe. In a world where we were expected to navigate adult responsibilities, misinformation filled the gaps left by the absence of real guidance.

My father had been an engineer at the telephone company—a man of precision, logic, and stability. His work required expertise, problem-solving, and a methodical approach to keeping communication lines operational. His world was structured, defined by blueprints, calculations, and the reliability of systems designed to function with efficiency.

By contrast, Doug's world was built on constant negotiation. He had the education and potential for a stable career—trained in accounting, a future in finance or business laid out before him—but he chose a different path. Managing an aging twenty-four room motel and working as a bookkeeping consultant for a private oil company was far from the life his degree could have afforded him. The motel was a revolving door of strangers, a place where people came and went, often leaving behind more problems than payments. Unlike my father's world of structure and order, Doug's existence was steeped in uncertainty, where broken toilets, overdue bills, and unreliable cleaning employees defined his struggles.

For me, life at the motel was an extension of the loss I had already endured. My father's death had forced me to grow up at seven, but the motel ensured I would never experience adolescence. There was no space for rebellion, no carefree teenage years, no gradual transition into adulthood. Responsibility was thrust upon me. By the time I turned fourteen, Doug and my mother regularly left my stepsiblings and me in charge of the motel while they attended social gatherings with church friends, visited Doug's parents, or ran errands for motel supplies. They framed it as an opportunity—a "real-world experience" that would teach us responsibility and business skills. But there was nothing empowering about it. Answering phones, renting rooms, and dealing with unfamiliar adults—some drunk, some angry, some just looking for a place to disappear—felt like an unbearable weight.

Unlike other kids my age, who spent evenings at football games, movies, or lost in the luxury of childhood, I was running a motel. The sound of the phone ringing sent a jolt of anxiety through me. Would it be a guest checking in? A complaint about a broken heater? Someone demanding a refund? Though nothing catastrophic ever happened, the pressure never eased. It wasn't an opportunity—it was a loss.

That loss, however, gave me something else: perception. The ability to see what others ignored. The courage to question what didn't feel right. The resilience to face truths others found too uncomfortable to confront. And though I was never safe—not in that motel, nor with my siblings and stepsiblings left exposed while the adults around us stayed unaware—I endured. That survival became my strength. It shaped who I am. It sharpened my instincts. And in the end, it gave me a voice.

One moment that still unsettles me began with what I thought would be a simple, joyful day. I had asked Doug and my mother if I could join them on a visit to Doug's parents, who lived on a farm about ninety minutes from the motel. I was eager to go—curious about their life, their land—especially since my sisters and stepsiblings all had other plans for the day. Doug's parents welcomed me warmly, and I spent the afternoon enjoying their hospitality: a table filled with homemade dishes, the comforting scent of freshly baked chocolate chip cookies, and the satisfying crunch of shelled pecans from the towering trees in their front yard. I felt, for a brief time, like I belonged.

But the drive back changed everything.

As the sun dipped low in the sky, Doug grew increasingly agitated, muttering about the work he needed to catch up on at the motel. He pressed hard on the gas pedal, speeding down the open highway at over seventy-five miles per hour. Suddenly, the piercing wail of a police siren shattered the quiet. Doug pulled over, tense. When the officer approached and cited him for excessive speed, my mother leaned across the front seat and said she was very ill—that Doug was rushing to get her to the hospital.

I sat in the backseat frozen.

The officer paused, looked her over, and then—believing her—let Doug go with only a warning. As we pulled back onto the road, a deep unease settled in my chest. I was shocked. Disappointed. Their lie had worked—but it had also broken something in me. I wanted to vanish, to fold into the air and disappear. If they could lie so effortlessly to a police officer, what else had they lied about? What had they told me that wasn't true?

My father had always valued honesty. His word was steady, grounding. In that moment, I realized I had expected the same from them. But now I couldn't help but wonder: How many other times had my mother feigned illness to get her way? Had I been falling for her stories all along?

Despite the motel's mayhem, I found an unexpected source of pride in my birthday. Born on Christmas Eve, I embraced the way the festive decorations, the twinkling lights, and the warmth of the season felt like an extension of my special day. In a world that often made me feel unseen, my birthday felt like a quiet acknowledgment from the universe that I mattered. I held tight to that sense of uniqueness, even as adolescence brought its own challenges.

Childhood memories of Christmas were magical in their simplicity. Before my father's death, our living room tree sparkled like a beacon of warmth and love, casting a comforting glow over our small world. One year, my mother gave me a small tree of my own—a gesture that felt personal at the time, as if she were carving out a space for me in the midst of the season's joy. I cherished that little tree, believing it was a symbol of her love.

Yet, as I grew older, I began to see the layers beneath her actions. My mother carried emotional wounds that she never spoke of that pressed against her spirit in ways I couldn't understand. Her compulsive shopping, the extravagant gifts, and the way she filled our home with material abundance were not acts of generosity but reflections of an emptiness she struggled to soothe. The gifts she gave, though grand, often felt hollow—an attempt to construct a closeness between us when all I wanted was her affection.

I came to understand that her love was tangled in her own pain. While I longed for something deeper—connection, reassurance, a mother who saw me beyond the pretty wrapped presents—I also learned to see her not as a parent but as a person carrying her own unspoken grief. And in that realization, I found a bittersweet kind of compassion—one that softened the disappointment and allowed me to hold both love and loss in the same breath.

The spring of 1967 brought a brief reprieve from the instability of our family merger when Doug and my mother announced plans to build a sprawling two-story Spanish-style house behind the motel. Watching the construction unfold filled me with hope. The finished home was a marvel—3,000 square feet of possibility. For the first time, I had my own bedroom, a space that felt like a haven in the midst of chaos. But the excitement of the new house came with conditions. Doug and my mother made it clear that the house was theirs, a distinction that reinforced my sense of being a guest in their world.

The house's grandeur couldn't erase the emotional divisions within our family. Meals were unstructured, often eaten alone, and the relationships within our blended household remained fraught. My bedroom became my sanctuary. I spent hours in the walk-in closet, a tiny space that felt like my own universe. There, I meditated and dreamed of a future that seemed just out of reach.

Paulie often came to my bedroom asking for rides to her friends' houses. Though I didn't mind helping, I knew what would come next—her relentless critiques. No matter how many times I drove her, she always had something to say.

One afternoon, as we pulled out of the neighborhood, she let out a loud sigh and crossed her arms. "You take turns too slow," she muttered, shaking her head. "You drive like an old lady."

I tightened my grip on the steering wheel but kept my eyes on the road. "I'd rather be safe than reckless," I said.

"Safe is one thing, but you act like the car's made of glass," she scoffed. "And put your right foot solid on the accelerator while you're at it. It looks like you have half of your foot on the pedal."

Her words grated on me, but they weren't new. She had a habit of pointing out every little thing—my hair, my clothes, my choices in life. I tried to ignore her, but the constant jabs challenged my patience.

One evening, as I drove her to yet another friend's house, she turned to me with a smirk. "So, you really think all that school stuff is gonna get you anywhere?"

I exhaled, bracing myself. "Yes, I do. Education matters."

She rolled her eyes. "Please. You spend all that time studying, but for what? You think you're better than everyone else just because you read books?"

I clenched my jaw but refused to let her see how much her words stung. "No, Paulie. I have to have good grades to get into college."

She huffed and turned toward the window. "I don't know why I got stuck with two oddball sisters."

Her words weren't just critiques—they were dismissals, attempts to chip away at my confidence, to make me feel small. I had long since stopped trying to change her mind or earn her approval. But every comment, every scoff, deepened the emotional distance between us. And as much as I wished things were different, I knew better than to expect anything else from Paulie.

By this time, I had mastered the art of endurance—adapting to circumstances beyond my control and pushing forward despite the hardships. I carried my strength in silence, allowing others to misinterpret me while I remained steadfast in my sense of self. I refused to let my environment define me or limit my aspirations. Instead, I used every challenge as fuel to propel myself toward the future I envisioned—one built on my own terms, with a foundation of perseverance, self-awareness, and a belief in my ability to overcome anything.

Chapter 6

High School and the Search for Belonging

DOUG AND MY MOTHER decided that Sally, Jessica, and I would attend an all-girls private high school, while Paulie enrolled at a private elementary school with Ashley, Don, Jeff, and Dennis. However, Sally struggled in school and was transferred to a public junior high close to the motel during the spring semester. After ninth grade, Jessica and I convinced Doug and my mother to let us attend a brand new public high school drawn by the school's proximity to Doug's motel, freeing them from the burden of tuition for us.

The first year brought significant changes for each of us. Unlike the rigid and underfunded private schools, the public high school offered a top-notch learning environment. Federal, state, and local funding ensured well-paid, top-tier educated teachers and state-of-the-art facilities. It was the first school in our city to offer central air conditioning, providing a comfortable learning atmosphere. The school boasted specialized equipment, a planetarium, and wholesome lunches. The library, with its floor-to-ceiling glass wall overlooking an open-air atrium garden, became my favorite place to study, bathed in natural light and tranquility.

For me, school was a refuge. Despite adjusting to male teachers after years of women at a military-like school, I embraced the supportive atmosphere. My enthusiasm for learning remained undiminished, and I participated in class discussions, often jumping up like a jack-in-the-box to answer questions. Over time, I shed the rigidity instilled by my previous schooling and found joy in education.

High school was a source of constant inspiration for me, from the teachers who served as mentors to the camaraderie I shared with friends. Driven by my determination to attend college, I took on part-time work in the school cafeteria, saving every penny.

I also babysat for a wealthy family with five children, whose parents often took week-long deep-sea fishing trips with their friends. The job paid just fifty cents an hour—a modest wage by today's standards, the equivalent to about $4.80 an hour today. Still, I embraced the responsibility, knowing how crucial those earnings were to achieving my dreams. Every dollar I made was deposited into my savings account, a tangible reminder of my commitment to my education and future success.

Teachers like Ms. Morris, who noticed my struggle to see the chalkboard, encouraged me to get corrective lenses—a step that proved invaluable for my education and for my overall vision. Their guidance helped me grow into a more confident and mature individual.

While Jessica and I thrived at school, Sally struggled to find her footing. She gravitated toward loud music, motorcycle rides, and smoking cigarettes—a world far removed from the disciplined routine Jessica and I maintained. At home, Sally's unpredictable outbursts cast a shadow over our evenings, prompting Jessica and me to retreat into our schoolwork.

Though Jessica and I walked to school together, she distanced herself upon reaching the entrance, unwilling to be seen with me. The stigma of our blended family, my mother's drug addiction, and Sally's mental health challenges weighed on her. While she was social with me at home, she kept her distance at school. Yet, despite these tensions, Jessica remained a quiet source of strength—a confidante I could turn to when I needed comfort the most.

Paulie's journey unfolded on a very different path. She attended a private church elementary school before enrolling in the same high school that I had attended. Paulie never spoke to me about her feelings, leaving me unsure of how she felt about her childhood. However, her teenage years revealed a stark contrast to Sally's gentle, albeit emotional, nature. While Sally was sensitive and tumultuous, Paulie was headstrong and critical. Their clashing personalities often led to fiery arguments, with me frequently stepping in as the reluctant peacemaker.

Paulie's detachment from our father's memory was striking—she referred to him as "that man," unable to grieve someone she never knew. Unlike Sally, who struggled but remained in school, Paulie had little interest in academics.

Her aspirations were clear: She wanted to be a mother. She left high school during her junior year after becoming pregnant and marrying the father of her child. However, the marriage ended after their second child was born, leaving Paulie to navigate life as a single mother.

Despite the hardships, Paulie's resilience was undeniable. Determined to provide for her two children after her brief marriage, she earned her GED and started a private business from her home. Her resourcefulness and determination to build a life on her terms were inspiring. Yet, life separated us too soon to develop a deep bond. I loved Paulie but often wished I had known her better—both the bright-eyed girl I remembered and the strong, independent woman she became.

My mother's health cast a long shadow over our lives. Between her frequent hospitalizations, struggles with self-care, and battles with addiction, she became distant and unattached. Her neglect extended to both Doug's children and us, often prioritizing her own needs over household responsibilities. She seldom combed her hair, brushed her teeth, showered, or wore clean clothes, further deepening the divide between her and the rest of the household. Doug, though hardworking and well-meaning, was stretched thin, juggling his job as a bookkeeper, motel owner, and raising a blended family.

Outside of school, Jessica and I volunteered as hospital candy stripers, donning red and white striped uniforms. My curiosity about healthcare professions led me to the electrocardiography and electroencephalogram unit, where I found a sense of purpose. Over time, I accumulated gold bars representing my service hours, a testament to my dedication.

The summer of 1969 marked a quiet turning point. At sixteen—just old enough to meet the minimum age requirement—Jessica and I secured part-time jobs in the mess hall of a nearby military facility, where we served junior officers from an East Coast military college. The work was far from glamorous, but the lessons ran deep. Each day unfolded with the sharp cadence of military order—demanding precision, respect, and resilience.

The summer heat and humidity didn't dampen our spirits. Even the short drive to the base felt like an adventure. We were tested in ways we hadn't expected, learning quickly the value of hard work, responsibility, and adaptability. These formative experiences, grounded in resilience and guided by a quiet trust in something greater than myself, helped shape the person I was becoming.

Dressed in white food service uniforms, our hair pinned under unflattering hairnets, we stood at attention each morning while supervisors inspected us for soiled clothing, chipped nails, or signs of illness—infractions that could lead to immediate dismissal. The strictness felt suffocating at first, but our years in private schools had conditioned us well for rules and routine. I was determined to be a good employee, to follow every rule and meet every expectation. This job provided experience, and it was a step toward my future. I needed the money for college, and I was willing to work hard.

What I wasn't prepared for—and I never adjusted to—was the relentless bullying from one of the supervisors. It went beyond strictness, beyond the expected authority of the job. He singled me out with humiliating remarks, his voice dripping with disdain as he criticized everything from my work to my posture, sometimes even the way I held my head. No mistake was too small, no flaw overlooked. The constant belittlement eroded my confidence, turning what should have been a summer of independence into something far more painful.

Looking back, Jessica and I were underage, navigating a world that demanded more from us than it should have. Our days settled into a routine: serving food to officers and junior officers, clearing tables, and assisting with food prep. Jessica, with her olive skin and dark hair, had a natural charm that caught the attention of several junior officers, and she even went on a few dates. I, on the other hand, preferred to stay under the radar, focusing on the job and avoiding trouble. Being on the base stirred bittersweet memories of my dad, who had loved taking my mother, Sally, and me to air shows. The sight of planes evoked both pride and an ache of his absence. Our situation was not unique—many young girls find themselves navigating adult spaces before their time, shaped by circumstances beyond their control.

The relentless summer heat made the kitchen unbearable, but the walk-in freezer offered brief moments of shocking relief. One afternoon, I was assigned to clean the freezer's stainless steel shelving. Armed with a pail of water, a cloth, and a can of powder cleanser, I stepped inside, the cold air hitting me like a slap. My wet hands numbed, and as the pain became unbearable, I decided to take a break—only to find the heavy metal door wouldn't open. I panicked. I hit the handle over and over, my screams swallowed by the thick walls.

Desperation set in as I pounded the door with the cleanser can, sending a cloud of white powder into the freezing air. My body trembled, and memories of the moment of near drowning at the seashore after my dad's death filled my mind. I prayed, as I had then, for strength and a miracle. A calm voice inside urged me to try again. Summoning every ounce of strength, I struck the handle once more, and the door swung open.

Collapsing outside of the freezer in front of the senior officer's office, I was disoriented and freezing. He ran to steady me and made me sit while I caught my breath. I feared being fired for the mess I had created with the cleansing powder, but his concern lay in the near death I'd escaped.

I never mentioned this incident to my mother or Doug. My private school training had instilled in me the rule that I should never go home from school and discuss anything that had happened there, and I applied the same logic to the military base. I was terrified of losing my job and getting into trouble with them. Even though it wasn't my fault, I couldn't shake the feeling that I would somehow be blamed for what had happened.

The next day, I returned to work, bolstered by Jessica's encouragement. The supervisor apologized, showing me the panic bell they'd installed overnight in the freezer—a precaution born from my ordeal.

Though shaken by the situation, I realized I wanted to live. Much like my near-drowning incident years before, all of my doubts about my worth as a human and my capacity to take care of myself were overshadowed by my wanting to live, and even to thrive.

Graduating from high school marked the culmination of one chapter and the uncertain start of another. While I savored the personal achievement of earning my diploma, the heavy emotions of family tensions and grief lingered. My home life, though stable in appearance, often felt fragmented. Doug provided financial security but lacked time from his work to spend with his own children and me. My mother, overwhelmed and unable to care for herself, let alone Sally, was ill-equipped to provide the guidance or support we needed.

My dear teacher, Ms. Morris, remained a cornerstone in my life throughout high school. Her elegance, intellect, and calm demeanor inspired me. She embodied the strength and poise I aspired to cultivate, even as I faced the unpredictability of adolescence.

In contrast, Sally's rebellion against the rigid expectations of Southern womanhood—and perhaps against the life Doug had brought into ours—led her down a different path. It's hard to imagine Cher as a countercultural icon today, but in the late '60s she was, and Sally idolized her. Her fascination with figures like Cher Bono and her embrace of free-spirited fashion stood in stark contrast to the structured world I sought to inhabit.

Sally's grief after our father's death ran deep. She fell further behind in her studies, and her depression drove her to self-harm and to attempt suicide at least twice that I was aware of. These were painful reminders of her struggle—ones our family seemed ill-equipped to address. My mother's silence on the matter and Doug's stoic approach left me feeling helpless. I wished for the openness and understanding my father had always provided, but instead, the unspoken truths settled over our household.

Despite the challenges at home, I found solace in personal growth and meaningful friendships. I developed independence and a strong work ethic, determined to carve out a future beyond my circumstances. My closest friends were bound for promising futures, and their ambitions inspired me to dream bigger. Among them was Carol, whose determination to become a doctor set her apart. She earned a scholarship to a private women's college in Massachusetts and later returned to Texas to pursue medical school. Other girlfriends pursued careers in nursing and communications, setting a high bar for what we could achieve. The boys I admired shared similar aspirations, focusing their studies on becoming doctors or attorneys. Surrounded by such driven and accomplished friends, I was motivated to push myself further, believing that a brighter future was within reach.

During our high school years, Carol and I decided to register for tennis classes instead of the standard physical education classes. It was a mixed class of boys and girls, which added an extra layer of challenge and, at times, frustration. Before each game, our coach required us to run track as part of our warm-up. The boys, eager to dominate, often ran far faster than the girls, leaving me humiliated as I lagged behind.

However, when it came to tennis pre-practice aerobic exercises, the tables turned. I discovered a surprising untapped reservoir of stamina that allowed me to outperform both the boys and the girls. This newfound strength was empowering, and I began to see my physical endurance as a reflection of my inner resilience.

This made me wonder: Where did this endurance originate? Was it physical conditioning, or was it something deeper—something tied to my life experiences? Given the challenges I had already faced, I had developed a mental and emotional stamina that far exceeded my years. Perhaps this physical endurance was an extension of that—an outward manifestation of an internal fortitude forged through adversity, doubt, and survival.

It seemed that my resilience had always been present, but sports provided the first tangible way to measure it. Running, pushing through exhaustion, and excelling in an environment where others struggled mirrored my ability to persist through life's difficulties. The very act of moving forward—whether on a tennis court or in life—became proof of my strength.

In those moments of endurance, I felt as though I was running on something deeper than physical energy. It was sheer willpower, an unconscious determination that had been cultivated long before I set foot on that court. This realization reinforced what I had always known deep down: No matter the obstacles I faced, I had the ability to push through—because I always had.

Tennis itself offered more than just a fun extracurricular activity. The discipline and focus it required taught me valuable lessons about persistence and strategy, while the physical benefits of the sport laid the foundation for a lifetime of healthy habits. Exercise became a vital part of my routine, something I would carry with me into adulthood.

Years later, while working on Wall Street in the high-pressure environment of the financial district, those lessons of perseverance and grit resurfaced. Competing with ambitious men in my career often felt like running track against the boys in high school—they underestimated me. But just as I had proven my stamina on the court and during aerobic drills, I demonstrated my determination to succeed in my professional life.

My relationships added depth to this circle of ambition. My first boyfriend, Mark, introduced me to the thrilling sensation of being admired and valued. Our romance was innocent yet meaningful, filled with dances, phone calls, and handwritten letters. When Mark enlisted in the army, the physical distance and strict censorship of our letters made it difficult to maintain our connection. Despite this, the sense of self-worth he instilled in me lingered, becoming a quiet source of strength during difficult times.

Later, my relationship with Todd brought reliability and companionship. His humor and ambition mirrored my own, and together we navigated milestones like prom and college applications. These relationships, both platonic and romantic, reinforced my belief in the importance of setting goals and striving for success, even amid life's qualms.

Prom was supposed to be a magical evening, and in many ways, it was. Draped in a shimmering white silk brocade gown with a kelly green ribbon cinched at my waist, I felt a rare sense of pride and confidence. I had chosen every detail, hoping to embody the elegance and joy that the night promised.

But despite the sparkle of the evening, there was a shadow I couldn't shake—Jessica's absence.

She had decided not to attend, or so she claimed. The more I thought about it, the more her decision pressed on me. Was it because of me? The thought gnawed at the edges of my happiness. I couldn't help but imagine her hesitation, the way she might have weighed her reputation, her image, against the possibility of standing next to me. It stung in ways I couldn't quite put into words, the kind of wound that pride insists you ignore but that lingers just beneath the surface.

Even as I twirled beneath the glowing lights, surrounded by laughter and the hopeful hum of music, her absence felt deliberate, almost like a silent rejection. The thought made my chest tighten, but I refused to let it consume the night. Instead, I smiled, swayed to the rhythm of the evening, and reminded myself that this was my moment—a celebration of youth and the possibilities that lay ahead. Still, a small voice inside whispered, *"What was it about me that made her stay away?"* I never found out the answer, but the question lingered, shadowing the memory of that night.

The tension within our family was palpable, a complex web of grief, resentment, and unmet expectations. My mother's drug abuse was both a symptom and a cause of this disarray, casting a shadow over our home. Her frequent falls, slurred speech, and inability to function without assistance became a tragic routine. I had grown accustomed to witnessing her under the influence, though it never ceased to frighten me. But for Doug's children, my stepsiblings, these moments were both shocking and unsettling. I feel certain that they discussed their disdain for my mother among themselves as if their silence was a fragile attempt to maintain civility or perhaps a quiet acknowledgment that no words were needed.

Doug's children, who had known a mother who was educated, kind, and loving, looked at mine with scorn. Their longing for the stability and care they had lost was evident, and their disappointment must have been greater than sharp—it must have cut deep. Their mother had been everything a child could hope for, and now they were forced to contend with a stepmother who was absent and irresponsible.

I often wondered how much they suffered, not just from their own loss but from the anarchy my mother brought into our shared home. While I had grown up navigating her unpredictable moods and reckless choices, they were thrust into it without warning, left to grieve the mother they had lost while enduring the presence of one who could never fill her place. In many ways, we all suffered together—our pain different yet intertwined, bound by a household that failed to provide what we all needed.

Adding to the strain was Sally, whose mental health challenges often erupted into outbursts that unsettled everyone. Her unpredictable behavior compounded the dysfunction, creating an environment where tension simmered, ready to boil over at any moment. Family dynamics became a fragile balancing act, with small incidents triggering disproportionate reactions.

Yet, despite the turmoil, there was a heavy silence—an unspoken agreement to ignore the elephant in the room. No one acknowledged the reality of my mother's and Sally's mental and emotional illnesses. We tiptoed around the truth, pretending that if we didn't name it, it might not exist. But the weight of what was left unsaid added to the strain, forcing us to navigate the turmoil in isolation, even as we all felt its crushing presence.

As I approached adulthood, my inner world was a mixture of hope and apprehension. The Apollo 11 moon landing in the summer of 1969 offered a brief reprieve—a moment of collective awe and inspiration. It gave me permission to dream, to imagine a future beyond the confines of our broken household. Yet even as I looked to the stars, I felt the weight of the present pulling me down. My dreams of escape sometimes felt like betrayals to those still tethered to the past.

In this contrast of aspiration and adversity, I found resilience. The moon landing ignited my imagination and reminded me of the possibilities that lay beyond my immediate reality. At the same time, my family's struggles grounded me, teaching me the importance of endurance. I began to understand that hope and hardship could coexist, shaping a path forward even in the face of pain. It was within this tension that I discovered the strength to dream, endure, and grow.

Graduation was a milestone, but it also highlighted the absence of those I longed to share it with—my father, who had been my steadfast supporter; Sally, who had dropped out of high school during our senior year as her mental health struggles made it impossible to meet basic academic requirements; and the extended family who had distanced themselves after my mother's remarriage.

Sally was beautiful and often had boyfriends, but none of them were interested in a long-term relationship with her. Her circle of friends stood in stark contrast to mine and Jessica's, leaning into rebellion and risk, a reflection of her pain and yearning for belonging. As I stood in my cap and gown, a bittersweet wave of pride and sorrow washed over me. I couldn't help but wonder what Sally might have achieved had circumstances been different.

After the ceremony, in the stillness of reflection, I turned my thoughts to the journey ahead. Despite the pain and challenges I had endured, I carried with me a hard-earned resilience, and the determination to dream beyond my circumstances. With these lessons as my foundation, I felt ready to embrace the next chapter of my life.

Chapter 7

A World Apart: Love, Chaos, and Contrasts

∞

THE HOMES OF MY boyfriends felt like portals to another world—places where serenity and structure were the norm, an unfamiliar contrast to the unpredictable storm I called home. My mother and Doug had built the largest house in the neighborhood—an imposing eight-bedroom, four-bathroom structure that, to outsiders, might have seemed like a dream. But inside, it was a stage for chaos, where appearances often masked the contradictions beneath.

The house itself was not just big—it was filled with eccentricities. Six peacocks roamed the property, chosen for their exotic beauty. My mother and Doug saw them as a mark of sophistication, their iridescent feathers decorating the lawn like living art. But at night, their screams—like the shrills of a woman in distress—shattered any illusion of refinement. Neighbors complained. Police showed up. The birds wandered onto the highway in front of the motel, causing traffic disruptions, leaving my parents scrambling to smooth things over with authorities. To the outside world, we were an oddity; to me, we were an embarrassment.

Inside, our home resembled a small-scale warehouse. My family bought groceries in bulk—cases of canned goods, industrial-sized containers of bath tissue and laundry detergent, and a milk supply fit for a restaurant. Doug, shaped by his rural upbringing, ensured our freezers were stocked with butchered meat his father shipped from his family's farm. Practical as it was, this deepened my sense of otherness. My boyfriends' families shopped at normal grocery stores, stocking their kitchens with just what they needed for the week. In their homes, I found a world where life seemed predictable, where everything had its place.

Holidays magnified these contrasts. While my boyfriends' families gathered around modest meals, our celebrations were grand productions. Two oversized turkeys, countless side dishes, and desserts enough to feed an army spread across two massive dining tables. My siblings and I made sure nothing went to waste, but the sheer excess often felt overwhelming. What others saw as abundance, I saw as performance—a way to mask the turmoil simmering just below the surface. I longed for the intimacy I witnessed in other homes, where connection seemed to matter more than spectacle.

Todd, my steady boyfriend in high school, became my escape. On the worst days, he'd drive us to the harbor, where we'd watch cargo ships glide across the water, their steady course hinting at a freedom I craved. Todd listened without judgment, offering a quiet refuge from the storm I lived in. He had dreams of becoming a lawyer, a future built on logic and order—everything my home life lacked.

In my boyfriends' households, boundaries and structure were woven into daily life. Parents set curfews, chaperoned dates, and enforced rules. I was grateful for their involvement—it was love and protection I didn't experience at home. At my house, rules were fluid, often forgotten amid the demands of running a motel or managing a large and unsupervised household.

Our dates often took us to elegant restaurants or cozy private dinner parties, where I marveled at the calm of their homes. In contrast, my family's home—first the motel and later the house—was a place of constant motion, with chores and routines overshadowed by the next crisis. Watching the stability in their families left me yearning for something I didn't yet know how to name.

The sheer size of my family fascinated and overwhelmed my boyfriends. Coming from small, tight-knit households, they were bewildered by the noise and commotion of my world. I joked about it, referencing *Cheaper by the Dozen* to soften the reality, but behind the humor lay a truth I could not share. Our household's chaos was both a badge of survival and a burden, the cracks hidden behind a polished facade.

I found it unsettling when my boyfriends asked if I wanted a large family someday. Their questions prodded at a wound I wasn't ready to expose.

"Do you think you'll want a bunch of kids?" one of them would ask, their tone light but their eyes searching.

I laughed. "A big family? No, I don't think so." I waved a hand, dismissing the thought. "Two kids would be plenty for me."

They would study me, their expressions relaxing as if reassured by my answer.

Each relationship brought lessons, moments of joy, and glimpses of the life I hoped to build. My friends' and boyfriends' ambitions pushed me to envision a future beyond the motel's confines. Carol's career path to medicine, Todd's determination to become a lawyer, and my girlfriends' aspirations in nursing and communications reminded me that resilience and hard work could open doors. Even as I juggled the disparities between my life and theirs, I held on to hope—a belief that my past could become the foundation for a life of purpose and peace.

Looking back now, I see the stark contrast between their dreams and my own reality. While they planned for college, careers, and futures built on stability, I was navigating a world of uncertainty, where survival took precedence over ambition. The motel and our new house held more than just my belongings—they held secrets, struggles, and a childhood that felt more like an endurance test than a time of growth. My dreams weren't grand; they were practical. A home that didn't feel temporary. A life free from the instability that had shaped me.

I used to wonder if I was destined to repeat the cycle, if my past had already written my future. But hope was stubborn. I clung to it, even in the darkest moments, believing that one day, I wouldn't just escape the madness—I would build something different in its place.

Part III
Breaking Free and Thriving

Chapter 8

Stepping into Adulthood

THANKS TO MY FATHER'S military service, I was fortunate to attend college with the support of Veterans Aid. Among all my relatives on both my mother's and father's sides, I was the one to seek and attain higher education. Sally and Paulie dropped out of high school with my mother's consent, choosing paths that diverged from my own. Determined to create a different future for myself, I took full advantage of the financial support available for tuition. While it eased some of the burden, my journey through higher education was far from stress-free.

After graduating from high school, I enrolled in a summer English 101 class. The accelerated curriculum allowed no room for additional courses, but I threw myself into the challenge. My instructor, Mr. Yantz, was a frail, soft-spoken man well past retirement age. His persistent coughing fits often interrupted lectures, leaving us worried for his health. Some classmates mocked him behind his back, but I respected his quiet wisdom and dedication. His office, located across from our classroom, became a refuge for me whenever I needed guidance on assignments.

On the first day of class, he introduced a major semester project that would account for 80 percent of our grade. Overwhelmed but resolute, I headed to the library to plan my approach. That library became my second home—a quiet, sunlit corner on the second floor offered the perfect space for focus and reflection. The natural light streaming through the windows and the stillness of the space became essential to my studies.

My days followed a strict routine: mornings attending classes, afternoons in the library, evenings at home to shower and sleep. The librarians became familiar with me as they ushered me out at closing time. Meals were simple affairs, often eaten in the car I shared with Sally and Jessica—a reliable used vehicle secured by Doug during our final year of high school.

While I dedicated myself to English 101, Sally pursued hairstyling, and Jessica worked as a cashier at a food market while planning to major in accounting. I admired Jessica's clarity of purpose; she had her sights set on becoming a CPA and was determined to succeed. She was following in Doug's footsteps, inspired by his career and the example he had set for her.

The semester project consumed my summer. On submission day, my heart raced as I handed in a three-ring notebook complete with a cover page, table of contents, and organized sections. Unlike my classmates' stapled papers, my project stood out. When Mr. Yantz frowned and remarked, "I don't want work from other classes," I replied, "This is only the work I've done for your class." He nodded, taking my notebook to his office without another word.

The following week during our final exam, he returned our projects. Before distributing them, he delivered a stern lecture on discipline, motivation, and the value of education. Then, to my surprise, he placed my notebook on my desk without a word. His softened expression conveyed more than any compliment could. At that moment, I felt a shift. After years of feeling overlooked and dismissed by my mother, I realized that my hard work mattered. I was capable of success. I was worthy of recognition.

The pressure to maintain good grades weighed on me. Unlike my peers, who often answered to their parents, I was accountable to the federal government. My Veterans Aid depended on my academic performance, and failure was not an option. My father's words echoed in my mind: *"Get an education. Get a good job. Take care of yourself."* These words became my mantra as I worked toward a future I had spent my childhood daring to imagine.

That summer was a trial of challenges that tested my determination. I faced the demands of college studies head-on, grappling with the rigor of coursework while striving to maintain grades high enough to secure the Veterans Aid funding essential to my education. Each exam and assignment carried the weight of not just academic success but the fear of financial instability should I falter.

During the second summer session, I added a physical education class alongside my English studies, carpooling with Todd. He loved calling me a "career woman" swept up in the Women's Liberation Movement. But for me, it wasn't about feminism—it was about survival. I wanted to be self-reliant, ready to care for myself and any children I might have, regardless of life's uncertainties.

Adding to the stress, my mother's health crisis grew dire. Her hospitalizations became longer and more serious, pulling at my emotions and straining my focus. Her drug dependency and neglect had always been a shadow over my life, but during this time, they crystallized into a clear lesson of what I did not want to become. Her instability fueled my drive to embrace structure, discipline, and self-reliance.

The late summer of 1970 unleashed the fury of a major hurricane, leaving behind a trail of destruction that would forever be woven into the fabric of our lives. While Doug and my mother were working at the motel to accommodate the needs of customers, Sally, Paulie, my stepsiblings, and I were at home alone, left to weather the storm's fury on our own. When the winds died down and the rain retreated, we stepped outside into a world that felt wrecked. The air hung heavy with the scent of salt, damp wood, and something acrid—shingles ripped from rooftops, splintered fences, and the distant smolder of downed power lines. In our backyard, a stainless steel kitchen sink lay damaged and out of place, flung onto our property from some unknown home.

Our house had borne the brunt of the hurricane's wrath. Shattered windows gaped like vacant eyes, their jagged edges still clinging to the frames. Inside, rainwater had forced its way through every vulnerable crack, soaking furniture and carpeting. The once-familiar hum of the refrigerator was gone, replaced by a suffocating silence. As if the hurricane's rage weren't enough, numerous tornadoes spawned in its wake, tearing through the neighborhood and inflicting even more damage on our already battered home.

When Doug and my mother walked from the back side of the motel and into our house, my mother gasped as her eyes swept over the wreckage, her body going rigid before her knees buckled beneath her. With a strangled cry, she collapsed onto the floor, her hands trembling as they reached out toward the ruins of our home. The weight of the devastation crushed her, leaving her breathless, her face pale and frozen in shock. Doug and I rushed to her side, our voices urgent but gentle, trying to pull her back from the brink of panic. Around us, the storm's aftermath loomed like a cruel specter, its destruction not just of wood and brick but of the fragile sense of safety we had clung to. Upstairs, Sally's piercing scream cut through the heavy air as the shattered window of her bedroom let the rain drench everything she held dear, an echo of the heartbreak that gripped us all.

Then came the heat.

With the power out for three relentless weeks, the sweltering Texas sun pressed down on us, unyielding. Days blurred together in a haze of sweat and exhaustion. The nights were no better—a thick, oppressive darkness, broken by the flickering beam of a flashlight casting creepy shadows on the walls. Without air conditioning, our bodies clung to the bedsheets, sweat pooling in the creases of our skin. We fanned ourselves, desperate for even the weakest whisper of cool air. The damp, stagnant air inside the house grew rank as mildew crept into the walls, the carpets, the furniture. Normalcy was nowhere to be found.

The National Guard patrolled the streets, enforcing a strict curfew that kept residents indoors past sunset. Their presence was a stark reminder that even as the winds had passed, the storm's grip on our lives remained unbroken. The hurricane had come and gone in a matter of hours, but the storm it left behind—inside our home, inside *us*—lingered far longer.

As I look back on that time in my life, I understand that Doug had to work. The motel was his livelihood—the means by which he kept food on our table and a roof over our heads. But abandoned in our home during the hurricane's destruction, I couldn't help but wish he had chosen differently. I wanted my mother and Doug to see *us*—their children—as their greatest priority, more important than the guests needing fresh linens or a stocked bathroom. I longed for their presence, for the reassurance that our safety mattered more than the demands of strangers passing through. The motel sustained us, but at what cost?

When I returned to campus, the darkness of the powerless buildings wrapped around me like a heavy shroud. The soft glow of candlelight flickered across the tables, casting long shadows as librarians handed out flashlights to weary students. I huddled over my books, the quiet hum of whispered conversations and rustling pages filling the space where fluorescent lights had once buzzed overhead.

By late August, Jessica embarked on her college journey at Rio Grande State University, while I remained at a local community college, balancing my studies with the growing weight of responsibility. Todd's father, a department director, helped me secure a part-time job in the Printing Office, where I collated stacks of class handouts and exams—the steady rhythm of shuffling paper grounding me in a much-needed routine. The pay was modest, but each dollar tucked into my savings strengthened my independence—proof that, despite the storm's attempt to break me, I was still standing.

By the spring semester, my mother's health had taken a sharp decline. At forty-one, her prescription drug abuse led to kidney failure, requiring expensive dialysis treatments. Access to the lifesaving therapy was limited, and her condition added another layer of tension to our already strained lives. Over time, my family's repeated panic over her health crises desensitized me.

Jessica's invitation to visit her at Rio Grande State University toward the end of the spring semester felt like an unexpected gift, a small gesture that hinted at the connection I had always hoped to share with her. As I helped her pack for the summer, she suggested that I apply to transfer for my sophomore year. The idea lit a spark in me—an opportunity for a fresh start, a chance to be part of something bigger.

Encouraged by her words, I submitted my application. When my acceptance letter arrived, I was overjoyed, filled with the hope that this move would bring me closer to Jessica, not in distance but in the bond I had longed for. But as I settled into campus life, it became clear that some things had not changed. As she had done in high school, Jessica kept me at arm's length, careful not to acknowledge our connection in front of her friends. Whether it was the way she never nodded in passing or how she avoided making plans when others were around, her message was clear—she didn't want to be associated with me, at least not in public.

The excitement I had felt at the start of this new chapter gave way to disappointment. I had imagined us growing closer, sharing late-night talks, and navigating college life together. Instead, I remained on the outside looking in, as I always had. During the summer break, I worked full time as a Volunteer Auxiliary Supervisor at the hospital where I had once been a candy striper, diligently saving every penny for college expenses.

Rio Grande State University, nestled in the Texas Hill Country, became my new academic home in the fall of 1971. When the semester began, I moved into Ashwood Hall and found myself sharing a room with Carolyn, a quiet but kind-hearted girl from Kendleton, Texas. From the start, she was a steady presence—never overbearing, never intrusive, but always there in the small, reassuring ways that mattered.

I didn't grasp the depth of her kindness until the night the flu hit me hard. Feverish and weak, I lay curled in bed, too exhausted to even think about seeking help. Carolyn noticed my worsening condition right away. Without hesitation, she insisted on taking me to the Student Health Center in the middle of the night.

But it wasn't just the act of getting me to the clinic that touched me—it was everything unspoken. The way she waited beside me as I drifted in and out of fevered exhaustion. The way she spoke to the nurse on my behalf when I was too weak to explain myself. The way she made sure I had everything I needed once we got back to our dorm, checking on me with genuine care that I had not experienced in many years.

In that moment, Carolyn became more than just a roommate—she was someone who saw me, someone who cared. And that, more than anything, left an imprint on me.

Living in a large, blended family had prepared me for the dynamics of dorm life. The house that Doug and my mother built often felt more like a college dormitory than a home, with constant activity, shared spaces, and little privacy. Growing up in that environment taught me the importance of respecting others' space and the value of boundaries—skills that served me well as I navigated the close quarters of Ashwood Hall.

Though the transition to college life came with its challenges, I found comfort in the familiar rhythm of a bustling, communal atmosphere. The constant hum of voices in the hallway and the unspoken give-and-take of dorm living felt less like an adjustment and more like a continuation of what I had always known.

Growing up, I had learned to navigate shifting dynamics, to find my place within ever-changing circumstances. Whether it was blending into a new household, respecting unspoken rules, or adapting to different personalities, my upbringing had instilled in me the ability to coexist with others. I understood when to step forward and when to step back, when to assert myself and when to yield.

That resilience made dorm life feel natural. While others struggled with negotiating differences, I moved with ease within it, using intuition to read situations and finding ways to belong without forcing my presence. College may have been a new chapter, but in many ways, I had been preparing for it my entire life.

At first, I pursued nursing, and I took a basic food and nutrition course that shifted my perspective. After discussions with Mrs. Hensley, one of my professors, I decided to pursue a degree in therapeutic dietetics, transferring to Western Meridian University. I wanted to focus on promoting health through nutrition rather than treating illness—a decision shaped by my parents' struggles and my desire for a healthier future.

That summer, I took a meaningful step toward my new career path by working as a dietitian assistant at the hospital where my father had once been a patient during his illness. Rotating through various units, I gained invaluable hands-on experience in therapeutic dietetics, confirming my decision to shift from nursing to promoting health through nutrition. The position helped offset the cost of my education.

In August, I made the drive to Western Meridian University, set in the wide-open panhandle region of Texas. The seven-and-a-half-hour drive from home in my secondhand, non-air-conditioned car—a bare-bones vehicle that was little more than a steering wheel and four tires—was grueling. The endless Texas highways, lined with rows of telephone poles, stretched ahead like a never-ending mirage, leaving me alone with my thoughts. In spite of the heat, dust, and the constant worry that my car might leave me stranded, I remained optimistic, focusing on my gratitude for the opportunity Veterans Aid benefits had provided.

When I arrived on campus, I checked into my new dormitory. Unpacking my car required multiple trips, and seeing other students accompanied by their families reminded me of my independence. At the same time, it reminded me of my father—I wanted him with me and to feel proud that I had followed his advice to get a good education. Still, I embraced this transition with confidence, viewing it as another step toward adulthood.

Western Meridian felt like home from the start. From the moment I set foot on campus, I was struck by a sense of warmth that extended beyond the West Texas sun. The university's reputation set it apart—it lacked the rowdy party-school culture that defined so many other campuses, and its dry county status reinforced a career-driven environment. Here, students were focused, determined, and ready to build their futures. That mindset suited me. I didn't feel like an outsider struggling to find my place—I felt like I had stepped into a community that understood and embraced my ambitions.

What eased my transition, though, was the unmistakable Texas hospitality. Professors took the time to learn my name, their doors open to discussions that extended beyond the classroom. Staff members greeted me with warm smiles, always ready to offer guidance or a kind word. Even the students embodied that welcoming spirit—strangers held doors open, offered directions without hesitation, and struck up conversations as if we had known each other for years.

I often had to take the university bus to get to my classes, and during peak hours, it was packed with students, leaving little room to move, let alone find a seat. But time and again, something happened that left me over the moon—if I boarded and the seats were full, a boy would stand up without hesitation and offer me his seat. It wasn't just politeness; it was a small but significant act of kindness that spoke volumes about the character of the students around me. Each time it happened, I was both impressed and touched.

There was an unspoken camaraderie that made the university feel less like an institution and more like a home. The red-brick buildings, the wide-open sky, and the steady hum of life on campus all contributed to a feeling of belonging I had never quite experienced before. Here, I wasn't just another student—I was part of something greater, a place where I could grow, thrive, and belong.

During holiday breaks, I flew home to visit family and Todd. Despite these visits, my time at college created a growing sense of detachment from home. Returning to campus for the start of the spring semester, I encountered snow for the first time. My institutional food management lab class started at 6:00 a.m., and it was still dark outside. Unaware of how dangerous winter weather could be, I couldn't see the thin layer of ice that had coated the cement steps outside my dorm.

I slipped, and in an instant, my body slammed hard onto the unforgiving concrete. I landed face down and couldn't move. A sharp, searing pain radiated from my lower back, leaving me terrified. As I lay there, frozen in place by both the cold and the pain, a storm of thoughts surged through my mind. *What if I couldn't walk again? What if this injury kept me from finishing my degree?* I had fought so hard to get into college—every test, every application, every obstacle I had overcome—and now it all felt like it was hanging in the balance.

Students appeared within seconds, rushing to help. Some took off their coats and gently laid them over me, their kindness and urgency cutting through the cold. I remember the voices—calm, concerned—trying to comfort me until the paramedics arrived.

When the paramedics kneeled beside me and asked if I could wiggle my toes, I focused, holding my breath, and managed a slight movement. Relief mixed with fear—I wasn't paralyzed, but I still didn't know the full extent of the damage. Tears streamed down my face as I was lifted onto a stretcher. I was then wheeled toward the waiting ambulance as terror settled deep in my chest.

I was lucky to have avoided serious injury. This experience, though unexpected and frightening, served as a lesson in adapting to winter weather. It introduced me to the reality of navigating cold climates, something that would become relevant in my later years living in the Northeast. The emotional aspect of feeling detached from home during college strengthened my toughness, but it was moments like this—being cared for and carried by the kindness of strangers—that reminded me I wasn't alone.

The university's expansive two-thousand-acre campus became a place of inspiration and growth. Strolling across its flat terrain offered both exercise and chances to connect with new people. Yet, it was the library that became my sanctuary—a quiet, welcoming refuge from the demands of student life. In its stillness, I felt safe, secure, and at my best. Here, I accomplished my work and also found a sense of comfort and protection that made all the difference.

Later that spring, Todd invited me to join his family on a summer trip to Grand Canyon National Park. The idea excited me—it promised adventure, a change of pace, and a chance to deepen my bond with Todd.

After finals, I packed my car for the drive home. Two hours south of the university, the engine suddenly sputtered and died, leaving me stranded in the middle of a desolate stretch of land. At first, I feared the worst— that the engine itself had failed—but it turned out the real culprit was the radiator. It had overheated and given out, causing the engine to stall. With no other options, I set out on foot in search of help and came upon a mental institution. An employee there kindly called for a tow truck, but as I waited, an unexpected wave of emotion washed over me.

I couldn't stop thinking about Sally. Deep down, I had always known she would one day end up in a place like this—tucked away from the world, where people's struggles were too often dismissed or forgotten. Standing outside, I imagined how isolating it must feel to be behind those walls, longing to be understood. A deep sense of empathy settled over me, sharper and heavier than before.

My car was repaired and I resumed my trip. But I carried something else with me—more than just gratitude for the strangers who had helped me. I carried a renewed commitment to see and acknowledge those who, like Sally, were too often unseen.

On my way home, I stopped to visit Nanny and Pappy for the first time in years. Nanny, ever supportive yet traditional, expressed concerns that my education might hinder my chances of finding a husband.

Nanny was, however, a remarkable woman. A self-taught seamstress and gardener, she designed and sewed wedding attire, cultivated orchids, and ran her own business while managing her household. Yet, societal norms of the time often diminished her contributions as mere "women's work." Her passing seven months later marked the end of an era, leaving me with lasting memories of her quiet strength and resourcefulness.

Nanny died of heart disease, but I always felt she also died of a broken heart. The early death of her husband in his forties; the loss of her third child, a daughter, six months after birth; the passing of her son—my father—at age thirty-two; and the painful separation from her three grandchildren by my mother whittled away at her spirit. Despite her resilience, the losses left a deep sorrow.

That summer, financial limitations closed one door but opened another—one that led to an unexpected journey across the Southwest. A part-time summer job managing banquets, highly recommended by one of my professors, seemed like a step toward stability—a chance to build something lasting. But without benefits and lacking the financial means to afford an apartment, the opportunity quickly slipped away. Instead, I joined Todd's family on a road trip to the Grand Canyon—a detour that would shape my future in ways I didn't yet realize.

From home, we traveled west, each mile unfurling before me like an invitation to something greater. San Antonio. El Paso. Tucson. Phoenix. Camelback Mountain, its silhouette as striking as its name. Flagstaff, crisp with pine-scented air. And then, the South Rim of the Grand Canyon—a place so vast, so humbling, that it felt like standing at the edge of possibility itself.

Somewhere along the way, Todd joked about moving to Los Angeles. I laughed, but the idea sank deeper into me than he could have imagined. LA had never been just a dream; it was a certainty, a quiet but persistent calling. This trip, in so many ways, felt like a dress rehearsal for the journey I would take alone years later.

On the return trip, we wound our way through Mesa Verde, past ancient cliff dwellings that whispered of endurance and strength, then crossed the vast, sacred lands of the Navajo Nation. We continued on to the Painted Desert, where the sun stretched long, golden shadows across the rippling earth. I took in every view, every shifting hue of the desert's palette—but my thoughts raced west, in the opposite direction. Though my eyes were fixed on the present landscape, my heart was already tethered to a skyline I had never seen. Los Angeles wasn't just a destination; it was a calling—a life I knew I was meant to claim.

Returning home, I knew with certainty that my path wouldn't end there. The trip had solidified what I had always felt but never articulated. I belonged in Los Angeles. And one day, I would make it my home.

Todd and I shared our final weeks together before my return to college. During one of our dates, he suggested we start seeing other people. His words hit me like a thunderbolt—unexpected and devastating. Though my heart was breaking, I managed to smile and thank him for the evening, hiding my anguish behind a mask of composure.

Once I was home, the emotions came flooding out. I locked myself in my room and cried until exhaustion took over.

"Why doesn't anyone love me?"

"What's wrong with me?"

"Am I not good enough? Not pretty enough? Not smart enough?"

"What am I doing wrong?"

The questions echoed through my mind. But even in my pain, I refused to let the heartbreak define me. I channeled my energy into preparing for my senior year, determined to focus on the future.

This was a turning point. I realized I was on my own now. While my heart ached, I appreciated that Todd gave me the space and freedom to step forward in my life as an adult. It was time to rebuild, heal, and embrace the next chapter of my life.

In the days leading up to my departure for college, I focused on packing and tying up loose ends at work. Each item I placed in my car represented another step toward the independence I craved and the future I was building. On the morning of my trip, as I was about to leave, Todd called. His voice carried an air of hesitation, as though he wanted to say more than he did. Though I kept our conversation brief, annoyance bubbled beneath the surface—why wait until the last minute to reach out? His suggestion to see other people still weighed on me, and I couldn't untangle his intentions. Channeling my frustration into thoughts of my studies, I leaned on a coping mechanism I had mastered since childhood: Focus on the tangible, the achievable, and leave the emotional confusion behind.

The drive back to college provided ample time for reflection. Alone with my thoughts, I resolved to take Todd's advice. If he wanted me to date others, I would give it a real chance—even if it was reluctant and bittersweet. Somewhere during the trip, I reasoned that Todd might have already found someone else and didn't know how to tell me. The thought hurt, but I used the ache as fuel to refocus on my goals. By the time I arrived at my dorm, my resolve had solidified: This year would be about my education and finding clarity for myself, not anyone else.

Back on campus, the rhythm of senior-level nutrition courses consumed my attention. My experience as a dietitian assistant gave the material new significance, making me eager to use the practical knowledge I had gained. Meanwhile, Todd's letters arrived with regularity, but I took my time to respond. I felt a widening emotional distance with each passing day. In one letter, he joked about how sudden I'd ended our phone call before leaving home: "Bye! I'm off to school!" His attempts at humor did little to resolve the tension lingering between us, and I wasn't ready to bridge that gap.

A week before Christmas break, a chance meeting with Brad marked the beginning of an unexpected turn in my life. A fourth-year medical student from Oklahoma, Brad stood out with his tall, slender frame, rusty red hair, and calm confidence. His path toward becoming a cardiologist and his background in pharmacology both impressed and intrigued me. When he asked for my telephone number, I felt a spark of curiosity but held no expectations.

Over the holidays, Todd asked me on a date. The dynamic between us had shifted. Todd, once a listener, now dominated the conversation, leaving little room for connection. When he asked if I was seeing other guys, I told him the truth: I was overwhelmed with school assignments. What I didn't share was my decision to remain open to new relationships, even if I still wasn't sure what I was looking for. As we sat in the awkward silence of his car, the unspoken words pressed between us like a weight too heavy to lift. By the time Todd drove me home, I felt a quiet finality settle in. That night, I retreated to my bedroom, comforted by the thought of returning to school and the forward momentum it offered.

After the spring semester began, Brad called, and we began dating. Todd's letters and long-distance calls persisted, but my interest waned. My roommate, Kathy, often ended up chatting with him, as I was most often out with Brad or buried in my studies. On Valentine's Day, Brad surprised me with a bouquet of red roses. I appreciated the gesture but felt self-conscious as the other girls in the dorm speculated about the sender. Kathy assumed they were from Todd, and I let her believe it. I preferred to keep my thoughts—and my budding relationship with Brad—private.

Brad brought excitement into my life. His thoughtful gestures—dinners, flowers, and a jade necklace that seemed made for me—contrasted with the emotional uncertainty of my past. He offered support in ways I hadn't known I needed, from advice on resumes to help with car repairs. His confidence in my ambitions made me feel seen and valued. Yet, as our relationship deepened, I couldn't ignore a cautious part of me that remained alert to potential red flags.

One such moment of doubt came a few months after we had begun dating. On our way to see the premiere of *The Great Gatsby*, Brad casually mentioned needing to stop by the pharmacy where he worked part-time. The building was already closed for the evening, but he assured me it would be quick, using his keys to slip inside. As I waited alone in the car, an uneasy feeling crept over me.

When Brad returned a few minutes later—empty-handed—his explanation felt thin, lacking truth. He had needed to check something, he said. But what? And why now, after hours? The questions stirred in my mind, uneasy and persistent.

My mother's dependence on prescription drugs had shaped my childhood in ways I never spoke about, and now, a troubling thought took hold: Was Brad, a pharmacist, using prescription drugs for reasons beyond his profession? I pushed the suspicion aside, unwilling to confront what it might mean. But the moment lingered, a quiet warning that not everything Brad said or did was as it seemed.

By December 1974, I had completed my coursework, days before my twenty-third birthday. Veterans Aid benefits had made this milestone possible, and though many classmates planned to celebrate by walking the stage in May 1975, I opted out.

The idea of sitting among thousands of strangers felt isolating, and the thought of celebrating alone seemed hollow. Brad was in Detroit, completing his medical school residency and unable to take time off to attend my graduation. Instead, I requested that the university mail my diploma. As I held it in my hands, I felt a profound mix of pride and determination. It was more than a piece of paper—it was a testament to the hard work, dedication to my studies, and my newfound independence that had carried me through every challenge.

Chapter 9
Early Career and Independence

MY FIRST FULL-TIME job as a dietitian was both a professional milestone and an emotional labyrinth. The position came with generous benefits—health, dental, vision, life insurance, paid sick leave, and vacation pay—offering financial security. Yet, as I walked the hospital halls, memories pressed in from all sides.

This was where my father had spent his final days. It was also where my mother's body had begun its slow collapse from years of anorexia, bulimia, and a dependence on prescription drugs. Her kidneys had failed, sentencing her to dialysis three times a week, a punishment she could not escape. The walls of the hospital had absorbed her suffering, and now, as I passed through them, I could still hear the echoes.

But my mother wasn't the only one swallowed by illness. Sally's mind had been rewritten in a psychiatric hospital a few blocks away. Desperate for relief, she had undergone experimental treatments that promised healing but instead erased entire pieces of her past—including our father. It was as if he had never existed in her world, his memory wiped clean while I was left holding every moment of his life and death alone.

The hospital had been the backdrop to so much loss, and now it was the setting for my new beginning. Each step I took was a quiet defiance of the past, a reminder that despite everything, I had endured.

This familiarity erased any sense of anonymity. My colleagues seemed to know more about my family's history than I was willing to share, leaving me feeling exposed and vulnerable. More than once, a nurse would glance at my name tag and say, "Oh, you're Sam Goble's daughter. I remember that he kept your photo by his bedside." Another time, a nurse stopped me in the hallway and said warmly, "Your father was Sam Goble? He was such a wonderful man. He always said thank you for everything we did for him."

Their words, though kind, only deepened the ache. It was as if the walls of the hospital carried memories of him I hadn't been ready to face. Visiting my mother after work added to the emotional strain—she was often too sedated for meaningful conversation. I stopped visiting, leaving her care to her mother and Aunt Audrey, who paid a visit more than anyone else. Doug, juggling both the motel and his tax consulting business, visited whenever his schedule allowed.

In the midst of the upheaval, I tried to distance myself. I clung to the memory of my father. His late-night wisdom and unflinching honesty became my compass, guiding me through the emotional turbulence that lingered long after his passing.

I could still hear his voice in the quiet moments when doubt crept in, steady and sure, reminding me of my own strength. When uncertainty threatened to pull me under, I thought of the times we spent talking—him on the sofa, me curled up beside him, hanging on to every word. My curiosity knew no bounds, from the simple act of learning to lace and tie my shoes to unraveling the mysteries of how the world worked. He never sugarcoated the truth, never softened the edges of reality, but in his honesty, there was always love.

He taught me how to navigate life's unexpected challenges with resilience and composure. One summer, while on a family trip to visit his relatives in East Texas, my father and I stood beneath an old apple tree, enjoying the shade. Without warning, an apple tumbled from the branches and struck me square on the head. The sudden jolt of pain and shock brought tears to my eyes.

My father, ever calm and steady, looked at me and said, "It's just an apple. Nothing to be afraid of." His words weren't dismissive—they were a lesson. In that moment, he was teaching me that not every discomfort was a crisis, that I was stronger than I realized.

From a young age, he instilled in me both physical and mental resilience, showing me how to endure life's bumps—whether they came in the form of falling fruit or far greater hardships. His belief in my strength became the foundation I stood on when everything else felt uncertain, his voice echoing in my mind whenever I was met with pain.

Even in his absence, he was there—his lessons woven into my every decision. When I stood at a crossroads, I asked myself what he would say. When my emotions threatened to consume me, I imagined his steady presence, reminding me to breathe, to think, to trust in my ability to rise. He had given me a map, not one drawn on paper but etched into my heart. And no matter how lost I felt, I always found my way back.

By 1975, I had begun to establish a life of my own. With my job at the hospital providing stability, I moved into a furnished apartment in a charming complex outfitted with modern comforts. It was the first time I had something that was mine—my own space, my own rules, my own life taking shape before me.

The apartment itself felt like a dream. The spacious living room became my sanctuary after long, exhausting days, a place where I could sink into the cushions and try to shake off the weight of everything I carried. The dining room gave me a sense of normalcy, a quiet spot where I could enjoy simple meals, even if I often ate alone. My cozy bedroom was more than a place to sleep—it was my retreat, a space where I could close the door on the outside world and pretend, if only for a little while, that everything was okay. The full mirror vanity dressing area, complete with a walk-in closet, felt like a small luxury, a reminder that I was building something of my own. The full bathroom, with ample storage, provided a sense of order amid the turmoil I often felt inside.

The practical amenities added to the comfort—front and back entrances for easy access, an assigned garage to keep my car safe, and a swimming pool steps from my door, offering a refreshing escape on warm days. But the best part was the location—a scenic seven-minute commute along the Gulf of Mexico, where the salty breeze and glistening waves gave me a brief reprieve from the heaviness of my days.

Yet, as much as I wanted to hold on to the joy of my newfound independence, the job that gave me stability also drained me. Working at the hospital was difficult. The long shifts, the suffering I witnessed, the weight of responsibility—it all pressed down on me, testing the very resilience my father had instilled in me. But I refused to break.

My hard work and dedication had placed me on a promising path in the medical field, and I was eager to see where it would lead. Around this time, Brad took a weekend break from his medical residency in Detroit to visit me. Like me, he was committed to his career in medicine, and it seemed we were both striving toward a future shaped by hard work, purpose, and compassion. With Brad, I felt a sense of connection and shared purpose—our goals, morals, and values aligning in a way that made the future feel full of possibility.

Two years into my role in the hospital's Food & Nutrition Department, I had become an integral member of the team, eventually catching the eye of its remarkable director—who simultaneously led the department and served as the Mother Superior of a nearby convent. Her incisive leadership and unwavering professionalism had left an indelible mark on me. I respected her immensely, admiring not only the commanding presence she wielded with both warmth and authority but also the rare balance she maintained between compassion and decisiveness. I considered myself fortunate to work under such an accomplished leader. Yet, one evening's encounter shattered that carefully built perception.

While securing a private dining room at the end of my shift, I walked in and saw the department's director and a priest in an intimate moment. Their startled reactions, though quickly masked by composure, sent a ripple of discomfort through me that I couldn't shake. It wasn't just the secrecy of their interaction—it was the stark contradiction between what I had been taught to believe about faith, morality, and leadership and the reality unfolding before me. I had been raised to revere religious figures as pillars of integrity, yet here were a nun and a priest—two individuals meant to embody the very morals I had been taught to uphold—entangled in something hidden, something forbidden.

The heaviness of what I had seen pressed down on me. I could tell no one. I had spent my life carrying family secrets—my mother's addiction, my siblings' struggles, the quiet shame that had always followed me like a shadow. Now, I was burdened with a secret from my professional life as well. It was yet another unspoken truth to bury, another betrayal to reconcile on my own.

As the days passed, my enthusiasm for my job began to shift. What once felt like a place of opportunity now felt tainted. The hospital, already tied to painful memories of my family's past, had become yet another place where truth was obscured by the need for appearances. The director still spoke with authority, still led with confidence, but I no longer saw her in the same light. My trust had fractured, not just in her but in the institution as a whole. My belief in organized religion, already fragile, now felt irreparably damaged.

I yearned to escape—to break free from my past, the contradictions of my present, and the suffocating silence that bound me to both. In my free time, I searched for job opportunities beyond Texas, poring over classified ads at the downtown library. During lunch breaks, I often sought solace in silent meditation at the hospital chapel, reflecting on the words my great-aunt Doris—my mother's aunt—had once shared with me in private as a child: "Get your education, leave, and live your own life." What once felt like distant, abstract advice now rebounded with clarity, illuminating my path forward. As a child, her words had seemed foreign and unreachable, but now their meaning was undeniable—I finally understood.

By October 1977, I made the decision to leave. I resigned from the hospital and drove to Detroit, where Brad was completing his medical residency. He supported my move, and within days of my arrival, I interviewed for a position at a local hospital. Confident in my prospects, I began apartment hunting and spent brief moments exploring Michigan's scenic countryside with Brad amid the vibrant colors of fall.

But one evening with Brad, I discovered a drawer in his apartment filled with prescription medications. My stomach tightened as I picked up one of the bottles, scanning the label.

Brad walked in as I turned to face him. I held up the bottle. "Why do you have so many different medications? This entire drawer is full of them."

He let out a small chuckle, shaking his head as if I were being naive. "Cynthia, you wouldn't understand. A doctor always has to have various drugs available for emergencies."

I frowned. "Emergencies? Brad, these aren't just basic first-aid supplies. Some of these are heavy-duty prescriptions. What kind of emergencies are you expecting to handle here, in your apartment?"

He sighed, his tone taking on a condescending edge. "Look, sweetheart, this is just part of being a physician. You're overthinking it."

The way he dismissed my concern made my skin prickle. I set the bottle down and met his gaze. "Don't talk to me like I'm a child. I know what I'm looking at. And I know what this reminds me of."

Brad crossed his arms, smirking slightly. "Oh, come on. You're being dramatic."

A tense silence stretched between us. His words ricocheted with the same dismissiveness I had heard too many times before. My unease deepened, pressing against my chest like a burden I couldn't shake. I exhaled sharply, knowing I wouldn't get the truth from him. But I didn't need it. I already knew what I had to do.

The next morning, I packed my belongings and drove back to Texas.

Brad later attributed my departure to homesickness, and I let him believe it. In truth, it marked the end of our relationship. Though the hospital where I had interviewed offered me the job, I declined. Despite losing both a promising relationship and a career opportunity, I felt no regret. My choices, guided by intuition and a commitment to integrity, reaffirmed my determination to build a life on my own terms. The path ahead was uncertain, but I trusted that it would lead me to where I needed to be.

After leaving Detroit, I resumed my search for a job. I chose California, where I was offered a full-time role as a nutrition consultant with an endocrinologist in Los Angeles. My start date, April 1978, left me just two weeks to pack, drive, and settle in—a tight but manageable timeline.

My decision to move was met with mixed reactions. My mother, displeased and resentful, made no effort to hide her feelings. In contrast, Doug offered quiet yet steadfast encouragement. On the morning of my departure, my mother refused to say goodbye, her icy demeanor cutting deeper than I anticipated. Doug, however, embraced me in a warm bear hug, his parting words a gentle reassurance: "You're going to be just fine." As I loaded the last of my belongings into the car, I couldn't shake a humiliating memory. Months earlier at the grocery store, my mother had remarked to a friend, "They leave, but they always come back." Her words, meant to wound, now served as fuel. I silently vowed never to return to the place I once called home.

I took the same route Todd and his family had driven during a vacation a few years earlier, tracing a path through San Antonio to El Paso, the westernmost tip of Texas. The seven-hundred-mile drive took me eight and a half hours, without the safety nets of a cell phone or auto club membership. Gas stations were scarce, and the radio offered little company. Despite the grueling monotony of the road, the breathtaking sunset that greeted me in El Paso made every mile worthwhile. It was the most stunning sunset I had ever seen—a celestial masterpiece painted across the horizon. In that moment, I felt as though I were gazing into the face of God. I felt a profound sense of comfort, as if God's presence was guiding and protecting me. I knew then that one chapter of my life was closing, and a new one was beginning.

That night, I checked into a modest roadside motel, ate a can of tuna from my survival kit, showered, and collapsed into bed. At dawn, I resumed my journey, driving six hundred miles through the unforgiving Sonoran

Desert. The oppressive heat, even in April, tested my endurance. Traveling alone in an older car heightened my anxiety, but I was prepared, keeping a supply of food and water in case of an emergency.

By the time I reached Blythe, Arizona, I was exhausted. I checked into another roadside motel, but something about the atmosphere felt off. The young male clerk at the desk, along with two other men in the lobby, seemed to be too friendly. After I brought a few bags into my room, the phone rang. It was the clerk asking me to join him and his friends. I panicked, declined, and barricaded the door with furniture. With no way to call the police without going through the motel switchboard, I spent a sleepless night, jumping at every sound. At first light, I left, shaken but determined to reach my destination.

Continuing west on Interstate 10, I passed through Indio, Thousand Palms, and Redlands before taking Interstate 210 North to Pasadena. Nestled in the San Gabriel Valley at the base of the San Gabriel Mountains, Pasadena felt like a haven. The cooler, drier climate was a refreshing contrast to South Texas, and the area's natural beauty made it feel inviting. The following day, I signed an apartment lease. Blue Allium decorated the courtyard, their delicate blooms lending a sense of tranquility. Surrounded by such beauty, I felt at peace.

I began my new role with Dr. Langford. Tall and slender, he looked to be in his early sixties. Born and raised in Nebraska, he and his wife had settled in Sierra Madre a decade earlier, drawn by the town's charm and proximity to Pasadena and the Angeles National Forest.

Dr. Langford's clinic was bustling. Most of his patients came from middle- to low-income backgrounds and sought treatment for obesity-related health issues, including high blood pressure, type 2 diabetes, and heart disease. My role involved consulting with patients after each appointment, helping them craft personalized diet plans and providing guidance on nutrition. At lunchtime, Dr. Langford and I often discussed ways to enhance our approach, focusing on appropriate, age-specific strategies to better serve our patients.

Though the job's benefits weren't as comprehensive as those at the hospital in Texas, the work was fulfilling. Patients appreciated my compassionate, nonjudgmental approach. I ensured they understood their diet plans and encouraged them to persevere, even after setbacks like overeating. Helping patients reclaim their health gave me a sense of purpose I hadn't experienced before.

Six days after starting my new job, daylight saving time began. As the clocks jumped forward an hour, I reflected on how symbolic this time change felt. I had fulfilled my father's dying wish and honored Great-Aunt Doris's advice to leave my birthplace and forge my own path. For the first time, I felt free. The chapter of my life tied to Texas was closed. I was thriving, and my future felt bright.

Toward the end of October, Dr. Langford had begun partnering with another physician, further adding to an already demanding schedule. Speculation swirled among the nurses and office staff that Dr. Langford might be preparing to sell his practice and retire. Although I avoided engaging in office gossip, I stayed optimistic yet pragmatic about the possibility of change. After all, stability had been a rare commodity in my life.

A month later, just after Thanksgiving, Dr. Langford confirmed the rumors: He was retiring and transitioning his practice to the new physician. However, the incoming doctor did not require my role as a nutritionist. Seven days later, I secured a full-time position in the Food & Nutrition Department at an oncology medical center. This private, not-for-profit clinical research center and graduate medical school was just a convenient seven-mile commute from my apartment. A significant portion of its multi-million-dollar budget came from charitable donations.

The medical center stood in stark contrast to the hospital in Texas, where I had previously worked. That facility had focused on general healthcare, treating a wide range of conditions, while this one was a hospital specializing in cancer and leukemia research. Patients were admitted if they qualified for one of the ongoing clinical trials.

What I didn't know at the time—what came as a complete surprise to me after accepting the job—was that this medical center had once been a glimmer of hope for my father. After physicians in Houston had exhausted every available treatment, his employer, the telephone company, had tried to have him admitted as a patient. I learned this through letters Aunt Dorothy and I exchanged, and I sat in stunned silence as I read her words.

With my deep-seated desire to help others, I found healthcare to be a natural and fulfilling career path. Making a positive difference in people's lives brought me purpose. My 6:00 a.m. to 3:00 p.m. shift suited my early-bird tendencies, and it worked well for my coworkers who preferred later hours. Together, the doctors, nurses, technicians, and I formed a dedicated team, united in our goal of improving patients' health.

However, the nature of the work took an emotional and physical toll. Many patients faced heartbreaking battles, often succumbing to complications from cancer and leukemia or being discharged with medications that carried the risk of overdose or suicide. Physician-assisted suicide was not an option, intensifying the emotional weight we carried. To cope with the high stress, the hospital provided resources to help staff maintain physical and mental well-being, emphasizing proper diet, exercise, and self-care.

While the medical center offered higher pay than I had earned before, the job was without doubt the most demanding of my career. One of the greatest challenges was caring for patients who could be irritable or difficult due to the side effects of their treatments. After six months, I received a promotion, though it felt more like a setback, as I was reassigned to the Head & Neck Surgery Unit and the ICU. Here, I witnessed experimental procedures that sometimes left patients bearing disfigurements reminiscent of Frankenstein's monster—not the Hollywood version, but a raw and real reflection of medical experimentation.

Being sensitive, I often bonded with patients, praying and hoping for their recovery. Their deaths weighed on me. On more than one occasion, I dreamed of them thanking me for being with them in their final moments. These vivid dreams, while a source of bittersweet comfort, left me drained. When hospital donations fell short, staffing cuts forced the remaining team members to shoulder even more responsibilities, compounding the pressure.

My duties involved working with patients who were in the final stages of their lives. Many had no effective treatments left to ease their pain, leaving me with the unsettling feeling that I was feeding the cancer rather than helping the patient. My shifts were spent on my feet, walking long corridors and attending to around thirty patients three to four times a day.

After three years at the medical center, I was assigned to the Pediatric Unit. The experience, though brief, left a lasting impression. One patient, a little girl named Cindy, cried for five days straight. Her frail body trembled with pain and fear. Despite the staff's best efforts, communication with Cindy was impossible. Feeling an overwhelming sense of compassion for her, I spent extra time sitting by her side as she cried. Her suffering mirrored the hopelessness I had felt as a child.

I retreated to a private restroom to cry, releasing my pent-up stress before composing myself, applying a fresh layer of lipstick, and returning to my duties. After one week, I requested to be reassigned, admitting that working with children was too difficult for me. Back in the Head & Neck Surgery Unit and ICU, I found it easier to manage my emotions while caring for adults.

Around this time, I met Rabbi Samuel Hirschman, the hospital chaplain. I sought his guidance, expressing my desire to study Judaism. My interest stemmed from living with the Horowitz family years earlier, where their kindness and faith had left a profound impact on me. Rabbi Hirschman agreed to teach me on Saturday mornings for three years. Unlike the other women in class, who were converting in preparation for marriage or motherhood, I pursued Judaism out of a desire to deepen my understanding.

During our sessions, I often confided in Rabbi Hirschman about the emotional challenges of working with dying patients. He shared his own experiences of suffering at Auschwitz, reminding me of the stark differences between his ordeal and the patients at the medical center, who at least had access to the finest medical care and comfort. Yet, from my perspective, suffering and death were constants in both places. I often wrestled with the question: How could God allow such pain?

In December 1979, I attended a Christmas Eve party. When asked where I worked, I replied with pride that I was employed at the oncology medical center. The room fell silent. One woman remarked, "Why would such a sweet person like you want to work in a dreadful place like that?" Others voiced concerns, asking if I feared contracting cancer. I explained that cancer and leukemia were not contagious. I answered them with truth, and despite my professional response, I couldn't shake the sting of their judgment.

Back at the hospital, I shared the experience with my colleagues, who reassured me that they had faced similar reactions. Still, the remarks replayed in my mind like a loop. I was used to rejection and exclusion, but this particular incident struck a nerve. I wondered if their reaction would have been different had I said I was a physician or scientist rather than a dietitian.

These moments of judgment and misunderstanding were difficult to endure, but they also reinforced my determination to remain steadfast in my work, knowing that I was contributing to something greater than myself.

Part IV
Finding Myself

Chapter 10

Pivots and New Beginnings

THREE WEEKS AFTER moving into my new apartment, I met Adam. It was a Saturday, and I had just returned from a much-needed grocery run to the food market.

After parking in the complex's garage, I grabbed my shopping bags and walked toward the common courtyard and pool. Three spaces from my assigned parking spot sat a sleek silver Camaro with New York plates. Something about them gave me pause, sparking an unexpected memory from childhood—piecing together a US map puzzle with Sally. I'd always been drawn to the New York and New Jersey pieces, sensing even then that those places would one day hold significance.

Snapping back to the present, I noticed a brown-haired man walking toward the Camaro. My gaze lingered on the New York plates as he approached.

"Hello, how's it going?" he said with a friendly smile.

I returned a shy smile. "Your New York plates caught my eye. I've been captivated by New York and New Jersey since I was a child."

We exchanged brief introductions, and I mentioned that I'd recently moved to California from Texas. He said his name was Adam and that he was pursuing a PhD in physics at a nearby university. Before parting, he suggested we pick up the conversation another time. We exchanged numbers, but I didn't think much of it at the time.

A few days later, Adam stopped by my apartment unexpectedly. Despite a flicker of hesitation, I invited him in. The conversation unfolded easily as he shared stories about growing up in New York, his experience as a pilot and flight instructor, and his drive to excel in his academic pursuits. While he didn't fit the typical Hollywood image of attractiveness, his intellect and quiet confidence carried a distinct magnetism.

Adam's mention over a dinner date that he was Jewish unsettled me because I was aware that Jewish practice discouraged relationships outside the faith. My Catholic upbringing, combined with a former Jewish friend from college, made me aware of the potential challenges of interfaith relationships. I had also lived with the Horowitz family, who were Reform Jews, during my father's illness, which gave me some insight into Jewish traditions. However, Adam was from an Orthodox Jewish family, where religious expectations were often stricter. This knowledge was concerning to me, and though Adam tried to reassure me that religion wouldn't be an issue, I couldn't shake my apprehension. His words would later take on a deeper complexity than I understood.

Adam led a fascinating life, earning the nickname "Whiz Kid" from our apartment complex neighbors. He thrived on adrenaline-fueled activities, from performing in aerobatic airshows to instructing aspiring pilots. Though his dream of becoming a NASA astronaut was thwarted by a color vision deficiency, he channeled that disappointment into other daring pursuits. A skilled pilot, he found exhilaration in the precision and thrill of aerobatic flying while also sharing his passion through teaching.

With financial support from his parents, Adam's life was a blend of privilege and unresolved emotional struggles. As the first male child of his parents, he bore the burden of their unspoken grief over the loss of a second child—a silence that shaped their family dynamics. Despite the obstacles he faced, he made the sky his domain, pushing boundaries both in flight and in life.

Something deep inside me hesitated, whispering warnings I chose to ignore. There were moments—fleeting but persistent—when unease crept in, a quiet discomfort that I brushed aside in favor of the intoxicating adventure Adam offered. He was thrilling, unpredictable, and unlike anyone I had ever known. His confidence drew me in, but beneath it, I sensed an undercurrent of something I couldn't quite name. Was it arrogance? Restlessness? A need for control? My intuition flickered with doubt, but I silenced it.

California dazzled me, and so did Adam. Our weekends were filled with endless road trips—the Golden Gate Bridge, Big Sur, the Sonoma Vineyards,

Disneyland—each mile pulling me further from the cautious voice in my head. The rush of new experiences, the sheer beauty surrounding me, made it easy to overlook the nagging sense that something wasn't right. I was happy, after all—happier than I had been in years. I had a good job, a beautiful apartment, and a life that, on the surface, felt almost perfect.

I told myself I was being too cautious, that my past had conditioned me to search for warning signs. But in the quiet moments, when the thrill of adventure faded, I felt the weight of what I refused to see. Instead of facing it, I convinced myself that love—real love—meant taking risks. So, I leaped, ignoring the part of me that whispered I was falling in the wrong direction.

Yet beneath the surface, there were cracks. Adam's charm often masked a manipulative streak, and over time, I began noticing his tendency to bend the truth to suit his narrative.

That summer, Adam and I took a road trip along Highway 1, a journey that felt like something out of a dream. From Santa Barbara to San Francisco, we journeyed through breathtaking landscapes and ended our day in luxury at a hotel nestled in Union Square.

At breakfast, a couple at the next table asked if we were on our honeymoon. Though we weren't, their comment made me blush with happiness. Before leaving San Francisco, we explored Golden Gate Park, drove across the Golden Gate Bridge, and dined at the iconic Fisherman's Wharf, indulging in freshly baked sourdough bread and decadent Ghirardelli chocolate.

On the drive back to Los Angeles, Adam proposed. I told him I loved him but insisted he finish his doctorate before we considered marriage. We had been dating for three months, and I was determined not to repeat my mother's mistakes by rushing into marriage. What I didn't know at the time was that Adam had been in a relationship with another woman days prior to me meeting him—news that would later cast a shadow over my memories of that summer.

Several weeks after our trip, I returned home one afternoon to find my apartment ransacked. Every unit in my corridor had been broken into. Shaken, I called the police—and Adam. The investigator suspected the burglars fled when I arrived, but the experience left me worried. Unable to secure my front door, I reluctantly accepted Adam's offer to stay at his apartment on the second floor of our complex. At the time, his place felt like a refuge, a safe harbor. But looking back, I see how fear and vulnerability nudged me further into his world, blurring the lines of my own independence. What felt like an act of protection was, in many ways, another step in losing myself. Now, with the clarity of distance, I recognize how pivotal moments like this shaped my understanding of trust, control, and the importance of standing on my own terms.

In late August, Adam left for a two-week trip to visit his parents in New York. As the center of their lives, Adam was idolized by his parents, who placed him on a high pedestal. While he was away, I kept busy. I compiled a scrapbook of all our adventures, collecting menus, postcards, and photos— anything to capture the magic of our time together.

I also wrote letters to Aunt Dorothy. Our correspondence had become a lifeline, offering a sense of stability in my otherwise uncertain world. Her letters each week were a reminder that I was loved, even when I felt alone.

When Adam returned, we picked up where we left off, spending every weekend together. But even as our relationship deepened, small inconsistencies began to surface. One day, I noticed Adam still had a New York State auto inspection sticker, despite living in California for years. His explanation—that his father mailed the stickers to him—didn't sit right with me. Years later, I learned the full truth: His father was orchestrating a scheme to bypass the California vehicle inspection process.

This revelation stayed with me, a sharp reminder of the differences between Adam's world and mine. My father, though present for a brief time in my life, had taught me the value of honesty and integrity. Adam's actions— and his family's complicity—highlighted a moral gap that I couldn't ignore.

By 1981, the emotional weight of caring for terminal cancer patients had become overwhelming. For years, I had drawn strength from helping patients through their most difficult moments, but witnessing so much suffering began to diminish my spirit. It wasn't fatigue alone; it was a deeper realization that, for my own well-being, I needed a change. Not a temporary reprieve from healthcare, but a transformation—one that would challenge me, fortify my resilience, and increase financial stability.

The insurance industry, which had been dominated by men, was beginning to open doors to women. My background in healthcare gave me an edge—an understanding of medical terminology and patient needs that set me apart from other candidates. Summit Guardian Insurance recognized this, and their western regional corporate offices in Los Angeles offered me an opportunity that, at first, seemed like a daring leap into the unknown.

Balancing both careers during this transition was a test of endurance, discipline, and sheer willpower. My days started at 6:00 a.m. at the medical center, where I worked until 3:00 p.m. Then, after a quick change from my hospital uniform to a sharp business suit, I drove to Summit's office in Pasadena for training from 4:00 p.m. to 7:00 p.m. My weekends were consumed by rigorous studying for the State Insurance Exam. Exhaustion was constant, but so was my determination. This shift was about more than a new job—it was about proving to myself that I had the strength to redefine my future.

By March 1982, my relentless efforts paid off: I had earned my life, accident, and health insurance license and accepted a position as an Account Executive at Franklin Ames Corporation, an independent insurance brokerage in Beverly Hills. I had realized a dream I'd carried since the fourth grade—to live in California and work in Beverly Hills.

Unlike Summit, where I would have been limited to selling products from a single company, Franklin Ames offered the freedom to work with multiple carriers. This flexibility allowed me to provide clients with the best possible coverage and aligned perfectly with my core values of personalized care and ethical service.

At Franklin Ames, I found incredible mentors in Robert Katz, the vice president, and Sophia Wilder, manager of Individual and Group Sales. Their guidance helped me navigate a new industry with confidence and precision. The company's president, Franklin Ames, managed operations from New York City, overseeing four branches across the country. It was a world unlike anything I had known, and I embraced it.

The challenges I faced during this transition were as profound as the achievements themselves. Securing over three hundred new clients in eight months was an extraordinary feat, but it came with immense pressure. The high-stakes environment of working with A-list actors required solid professionalism, adaptability, and discretion. Every interaction demanded confidence, yet I was still finding my footing in an industry vastly different from the one I had left behind.

Walking away from healthcare was more than a career shift; it was an act of survival. The decision carried emotional weight, compelling me to redefine my identity and sense of worth beyond the field to which I had once devoted myself. There was uncertainty—would I thrive in this new space, or had I taken too great a risk? The insurance industry pushed me beyond my comfort zone, challenging me to build something new from the ground up.

Yet, as I navigated these challenges, I uncovered an undeniable truth: The power to reshape my future was within me. Each policy secured was more than a sale; it was proof of my ability to adapt, succeed, and reclaim control over my life. This chapter of my journey reinforced my flexibility, proving that even in the face of uncertainty, I could forge a new path—one defined not by fear but by courage and self-determination.

Adam's graduation day in June 1982 should have been a moment of unfiltered joy—a crowning triumph after years of relentless dedication. He had earned his PhD in physics, an extraordinary accomplishment in itself, and was further distinguished by receiving a prestigious award for his dissertation—an honor so rare it hadn't been bestowed in over three decades. The day was picture-perfect: an outdoor ceremony held under cloudless blue skies, with temperatures lingering comfortably in the mid-70s. And yet, beneath the applause and ceremonial pomp, a quiet sorrow stirred—an unmistakable undercurrent that shadowed the celebration.

Adam's demeanor had been unusual in the weeks leading up to this day, and his reluctance to even attend the ceremony had left me confused. This was a milestone most would embrace with pride, yet he had seemed disconnected, almost resistant. His odd behavior a month earlier—the sudden declaration that he wouldn't go—lingered in my mind, adding to the unease that shadowed the day.

Looking back, I can see how I felt both his sadness and my own. What should have been a moment of shared joy felt hollow, weighed down by an emotional distance I didn't yet understand. His behavior was a warning sign, a glimpse into something unsettled within him. At the time, I didn't have the perspective to name it, but now, I recognize that my own feelings of confusion and sadness were more than reactions—they were quiet signals urging me to pay attention to the things left unspoken.

This struck me as strange—why would someone earning such an impressive honor skip their own graduation? I had assumed that his parents and relatives would travel to California to celebrate with him, but Adam assured me there would be no visitors, no reception, no dinner. Despite his resistance, I decided I would take Friday off work to watch him graduate. "There's no need," he said, dismissing the idea. "I'm not going."

Yet, the week of graduation, he changed his mind. Adam informed me that his father, Abram, would be flying in after all, though his mother and other relatives would not. His explanation was brief: Sarra, Adam's mother, stayed in New York to care for her own mother who was exhibiting signs of Alzheimer's disease. Her absence struck me as odd—she had also missed Adam's master's graduation a few years earlier. I kept my thoughts to myself, but the mysteries lingered.

The days leading up to graduation were tense. Adam's stress levels were palpable, making even casual conversations difficult. That week, I packed my belongings and moved them back to my own apartment downstairs. Adam didn't want his father to know we were living together.

The night before the ceremony, we drove to LAX to meet Abram. Stocky, balding, and perspiring, he radiated a self-assured authority that left little room for connection. He was the kind of man who treated his opinions as facts, expecting everyone else to fall in line. Within hours of meeting him, it was clear he was controlling and judgmental.

On the way back, Adam suggested we stop for dinner in Santa Monica, choosing a Japanese restaurant. It wasn't kosher—clearly not—but I said nothing. I wasn't sure if it was my place to ask why Abram, a devout Orthodox Jew, would want to eat from a kitchen that likely mixed meat, shellfish, and dairy, or if maybe I had misunderstood the boundaries of his observance. Was this an exception? A convenience? A double standard? The contradiction sat with me, but I swallowed my questions with the miso soup.

We sat at a communal table with strangers, which helped lighten the mood. The shared space diffused some of the tension that had been building all day, and for a moment, things almost felt normal. But even amid the small talk and clinking chopsticks, I couldn't ignore Sarra's absence. She wasn't there, and no one mentioned her. It felt deliberate, like a silence everyone had agreed to maintain. I wanted to ask: Was this about me, or something deeper within their family? The quiet surrounding her absence echoed louder than any answer might have.

Still, I said nothing. I told myself it wasn't the time, that bringing it up might crack whatever fragile calm we had managed to find in that room full of strangers. But the questions lingered, tucked beneath the surface of an otherwise unremarkable meal.

The next morning, I sat beside Abram at the graduation ceremony, surrounded by a crowd buzzing with excitement. Proud families cheered as their graduates crossed the stage, their voices blending into a chorus of celebration. As I scanned the sea of caps and gowns, my eyes kept landing on

Adam. His face was taut, his expression clouded with unmistakable tension. A knot tightened in my stomach—I couldn't shake the feeling that something was troubling him.

After the ceremony, Abram snapped photos of Adam in his cap and gown, using roll after roll of film to capture the moment. As I stood back and watched, I couldn't help but compare this scene to my own graduation. Had my dad lived, I imagined he would have been as proud, taking photos of me and offering warm hugs. But my own experience had been quiet and understated—no family celebration, no parties, a diploma, and a sense of quiet accomplishment.

As I reflected, an Asian student approached Adam, congratulating him with warm admiration. She introduced herself to Abram and spoke about her studies in physics at the same university. I stood nearby, but no introductions were made. I told myself it was an innocent oversight, the result of the day's excitement. A year later, I understood the real reason I had been overlooked.

As the ceremony concluded, Adam and Abram received an invitation to a reception—an invitation that did not extend to me. The exclusion stung, though I tried to push the feeling aside. Since I had driven by myself, I had little choice but to return to my apartment alone, the silence of the drive amplifying my disappointment.

Later that afternoon, the three of us set out on a scenic drive along the California coastline, passing through Newport Beach, Palos Verdes, Manhattan Beach, and Marina Del Rey. The breathtaking views should have been a welcome distraction, yet the unspoken tension lingered. The omission from the reception loomed over me, leaving me to wonder why I had been left out.

At sunset, we dined at RJ's Rib Joint in Beverly Hills, known for its legendary ribs and laid-back vibe. It should have been a celebration—Adam's graduation was a major milestone. But despite the festive setting, I couldn't quiet the ache that had crept in beneath my smile.

The food was undeniably good, but something didn't sit right.

Why are we even here? I found myself wondering as I glanced around the table. RJ's isn't kosher.

I stared down at the plate of saucy ribs, trying to reconcile the contradiction.

Why are Adam and Abram eating here? Why choose a place like this when they were raised in a strict kosher home?

The questions multiplied with each bite.

Why had Adam resisted going to his own graduation ceremony?

Why hadn't Sarra come to support her son, despite everything he'd accomplished?

And why had Adam introduced me to Abram as his "friend"? The word had landed with a dull thud.

As the evening wore on, the joy of the meal couldn't compete with the silence between the lines.

The next morning, we dropped Abram off at LAX for his flight back to New York. The airport goodbye was brief, but the moment he disappeared into the terminal, the questions I had buried all weekend rose back to the surface.

Was I missing something? Was this about something Adam hadn't yet figured out for himself?

There was something under the surface of all of it—his unease, the distance, the small choices that didn't quite make sense. I didn't know what it was yet.

Adam's invitation to join him for the 1982 Christmas holidays with his parents felt like a significant step forward in our relationship. He purchased our tickets, and though he left two weeks before I did, I would meet him in New York, and we'd return to Los Angeles together on New Year's Eve. Christmas Eve also marked my thirtieth birthday, and while I had hoped it might be a special milestone, it instead became a somber reflection of how I didn't belong in his family.

Arriving in New York, Abram greeted me with a curt handshake. Sarra was a ghost in her own home, flitting from room to room, catering and cleaning up after Abram and Adam while tending to endless chores. She seemed to disappear into the background, serving us dinner at the dining table before retreating to the kitchen to eat her own meal alone.

I followed her once, curious, and found her seated in the corner of the tiny kitchen, quietly eating a bowl of plain boiled macaroni with ketchup. The sight struck me—so stark in its simplicity, so unlike the warm, fragrant meal she had just served us.

"Sarra, won't you join us at the table?" I asked gently, motioning toward the dining room.

She looked up with a faint smile and shook her head. "I appreciate your offer," she whispered, "but I always eat by myself here in the kitchen."

Her hesitant demeanor was heartbreaking—a silent testament to the unbalanced and strained marriage she had with Abram. She wrung her hands and washed them with compulsion, over and over again. Her voice rarely rose above a whisper, forcing me to lean in and ask her to repeat herself more than once. There was something both tender and tragic in the way she moved through her home—present, yet somehow always apart.

The house itself was stifling—a hoarder's labyrinth of sentimental clutter and neglect. The air smelled faintly of mothballs, and Sarra wore threadbare sweaters and outdated clothing that had once belonged to Adam. Abram's car was as emblematic of their disarray, overflowing with crumpled fast-food wrappers and yellowing newspapers. The physical environment mirrored their emotional chaos—unresolved, repressed, and teetering on the edge of dysfunction.

What struck me most was their almost worshipful reverence for Adam. Sarra's chest puffed with pride as she regaled me with tales of Adam's childhood triumphs. To hear her tell it, Adam was a prodigy, untouched by flaw or failure. His bar mitzvah? Perfect in every way. His elementary school science projects? All his own doing, Sarra claimed, dismissing the efforts of other students who had partnered with Adam on joint assignments. Sarra added that even Adam's paternal grandmother, Lena, favored him above all her other grandchildren. The blatant favoritism wasn't a slight to the other grandchildren they overlooked—it cut into me as well, dredging up painful echoes of my own mother's indifference.

When Sarra tried to shift the focus onto me, she stumbled. "Cindy, dear," she said with awkwardness, "I'm sure your mother must be so proud of you."

Her words hit a raw nerve. The truth was too painful to admit—that my mother didn't love me, that I had never been anyone's "golden girl." Her well-meaning comment deepened my sense of isolation. The attempt felt forced, leaving me feeling even more like an outsider in a family I could never be part of.

I forced a tight smile, swallowing the lump in my throat. "I wouldn't know," I said, my voice quieter than I intended. "She's never told me."

Our conversation fell silent. Sarra's face paled, and for a moment, she looked as though she wished she could take the words back. I dropped my gaze to my hands, willing myself not to let the hurt show. The moment passed, conversation resumed, but inside, the ache remained—a silent, persistent reminder that some truths were too heavy to share.

Sarra, meanwhile, clung to her idealized vision of Adam. She believed he could do no wrong, even when his actions contradicted her rose-tinted perspective.

Adam's relationship with his parents was unsettling. To an outsider, he might have appeared charming and affable, but the cracks were obvious to me. He manipulated them with ease, disarming them with flattery or evasion and rebelling in ways that cut deep. Abram seemed to view Adam as an extension of himself. Their bond was symbiotic yet toxic, feeding each other's arrogance and dysfunction.

The red flags were abundant—Abram's domineering nature, Sarra's passivity, the excessive adoration of Adam, and Adam's own manipulative tendencies. Yet, I brushed them aside, dismissing them as cultural differences or harmless quirks. I told myself I could navigate the dysfunction, that I could somehow bridge the gap between Adam's world and my own.

By the time we returned to Los Angeles on New Year's Eve, I was drained but relieved to leave the oppressive environment behind. Still, an unease lingered, following me home like a shadow. It would take years—far too many—for me to comprehend the depth of dysfunction I had witnessed and how it mirrored, in its own way, the chaos of my own upbringing.

Chapter 11

Building a Life in New Jersey

∞

SPRING 1983 MARKED a period of transition. While I focused on building a future in California, change loomed on the horizon. Adam's fellowship at the university was coming to an end. He began interviewing for career roles in both business and academia, receiving offers from global defense and technology companies—yet neither seemed to ignite his enthusiasm.

Meanwhile, I was thriving in my career. Restructuring at the Franklin Ames Corporation had shifted leadership, creating new opportunities for me. Robert Katz, my mentor and the vice president, had been promoted to Senior Vice President and relocated to the New York City headquarters. Sophia Wilder, another trusted guide, accepted a position at a Santa Monica firm, leaving me to take on much of her workload. The added responsibilities challenged and energized me.

By July, Adam accepted a position as a tenure-track assistant professor in experimental quantum science in Department of Physics at a university in central New Jersey. His start date in late August left us scrambling to prepare.

Adam drove to New Jersey ahead of me, settling into university housing and preparing for his teaching schedule. Robert arranged for me to transfer to the New York City headquarters, allowing me to continue working under his guidance. My salary increased, and the company also covered the cost of my train commute from New Jersey to Midtown Manhattan. My new role was set to begin in mid-September.

In August, Adam and I packed up our belongings and sent them with a moving company. The last days in Los Angeles were uneventful—until a knock at the door shattered my perception of our relationship.

Adam stepped outside to answer it, and when he returned moments later, he was pale and trembling. Sitting on the bedroom floor, he broke down in tears—a side of him I had never seen. Between sobs, he confessed to an affair with another woman. Stunned but calm, I listened as he insisted it was over and claimed she was "crazy" and unwilling to let go.

Then came a second knock. This time, Adam brought the woman inside. Introducing herself as Eliza Wu, she stood with a composed demeanor and said, "I just wanted to meet you." Her audacity left me reeling, but I exchanged stiff pleasantries before she left. I recognized her as the Asian student who had approached Adam with warm admiration on the day of his graduation. She had introduced herself to Adam's father and spoken about her studies in physics, her tone bright with enthusiasm. Now, standing in our apartment, she embodied a piece of the life Adam had built without me— one I was only beginning to piece together. Adam reassured me the affair was over and promised a fresh start in New Jersey, even speaking of dreams we'd shared, like getting the bloodhound puppy we'd always wanted. Despite my doubts, I clung to his promises.

What I didn't know at the time was that Adam had left Los Angeles with Eliza, driving her to Iowa to visit her parents before he continued on his own to New Jersey. Meanwhile, I packed up my office, shipped the boxes to the company's headquarters in New York City, and left the Beverly Hills office behind. Then, I set off on my solo cross-country drive in my blue Toyota Corolla—a car without air conditioning, a cell phone, or even reliable radio reception.

The long drive gave me time to think. I was no stranger to rejection, but Adam's betrayal cut deeper than the rest. I had loved him, and despite the pain he caused, a part of me still clung to the hope that what we had wasn't lost. His deception cast a heavy shadow over the fresh start I was supposed to find in New Jersey, yet I pressed on, convincing myself that stability and renewal awaited me. Perhaps if I kept moving forward, the ache in my chest would fade.

The township where we settled was picturesque, with ivy-covered buildings and tree-lined streets, but to me, it was a cultural shock. I had traded the sprawling, sunlit ease of Los Angeles for a small university town that felt insulated and foreign. The two-bedroom university housing unit was three blocks from campus. On the surface, it seemed idyllic, but beneath that illusion, the fractures in our relationship were already deepening. His betrayal had planted seeds of doubt, and no matter how much I tried to ignore them, they took root. I wanted to believe in the future we had envisioned together, but the dishonesty, the inconsistencies in his words and actions, made it impossible to trust him. I second-guessed everything—his late nights, his excuses, even the way he said my name. It was as if I were watching our relationship from the outside, waiting for it to collapse.

Adam's unpredictable moods, his need for control, and his secretive tendencies were red flags I continued to ignore. He rented a mailbox at the post office, claiming it was safer than receiving mail at the housing complex. I also learned later that I wasn't supposed to be living there—Adam had lied to the university, claiming I was his fiancée.

One Saturday afternoon, a delivery from a local florist arrived: a large potted plant addressed to Adam. His reaction was immediate and unusual. He placed the plant outside on the porch without explanation and announced he needed to drive to his office. Weeks later, I discovered the truth: The plant was from Eliza Wu, the woman Adam had assured me was no longer part of his life.

On Monday morning, as I stepped into my New York City office, I shut the door behind me and leaned against it for a moment. My hands quivered as I reached for the phone, gripping the receiver with a mix of hesitation and determination. The hum of fluorescent lights overhead seemed deafening in the silence. I had rehearsed this conversation in my mind a dozen times, convincing myself that Eliza would have nothing to say that could shake me. But as soon as she answered, my resolve wavered.

"Eliza," I began, my voice steadier than I expected. "I need to hear it from you. What's going on between you and Adam?"

A pause. Then a sigh. "Cynthia," she said in a flat tone, "Adam doesn't love you."

The words landed like a physical blow, knocking the breath from my lungs. My fingers clenched the receiver so tight that my knuckles ached. "That's not true," I replied, forcing a firm voice. "Adam has always told me he loves me. He chose me, not you."

Eliza's voice was cold and unwavering. "The reason he's in New Jersey with you is because I'm here in California finishing my doctorate degree."

Her certainty made my stomach twist. I searched for something— anything—to counter her claim. But I could already feel the ground shifting beneath me.

"You're wrong," I whispered. "Adam and I have a life together. We—"

"You believe that?" she interrupted. "Cynthia, he loves me."

I wanted to hang up, to shut out her voice before it unraveled everything I had built my life around. But instead, I sat frozen, gripping the phone.

Eliza sighed again, softer this time. "I'm not trying to hurt you. But you deserve to know the truth."

I swallowed hard, my throat tight. Her words had cracked something inside me, but still, I wasn't ready to let go. I couldn't. So I did the one thing I knew how to do—I chose to believe Adam.

Adam's mood swings grew more pronounced. Some days, he was energized, speaking with admiration about his work and the university's prestige. Other times, he withdrew into brooding silence, his discontent hanging heavy between us. When I asked what was wrong, his answers were vague, often dismissive.

"Oh, I guess I'm just hungry," he'd say with a forced laugh. "I get that way sometimes."

But I knew better. His evasions weren't small untruths—they were walls, constructed to keep me on the outside.

Commuting to New York City added to the strain. The three-hour round-trip train rides left me exhausted. The city's relentless pace and gritty reality felt worlds apart from Los Angeles, making me feel vulnerable and exposed. Robert's advice about staying safe echoed in my mind, a constant refrain in an unfamiliar world.

In September 1984, Adam's career reached new heights when he won an Emmy for his cinematography work on *Aftermath: The Final Dawn*. It should have been a celebration, but Adam discouraged me from attending the ceremony in Los Angeles, downplaying his chances of winning. I learned years later he had gone with Eliza. The truth hit like a wound reopened— sharp, bitter, and personal.

I also uncovered the real reason Adam maintained a post office box. He had claimed it was for safety—something about the housing complex being unreliable—but the truth was far more telling. The box wasn't about security; it was about secrecy. It allowed him to receive mail from Eliza, the very woman he insisted was no longer part of his life. That seemingly random plant delivery, his strange reaction, and sudden departure that afternoon were the unraveling threads. In time, I would come to understand that Eliza's presence in his life never ended—and the post office box was a tool to keep that truth hidden.

The Emmy win seemed to amplify Adam's arrogance. His impulsive purchase of a black Buick Grand National, a turbocharged coupe, was a glaring example. The flashy muscle car felt out of place in the university's subdued elegance, and I found it embarrassing. But Adam reveled in the attention it brought, basking in the admiration of college students and teenagers.

He carried his Emmy to his office whenever visiting professors arrived at the university as guest speakers within the Physics Department, ensuring they took notice of his achievement. He wore a black jacket with the name of the film company emblazoned on the back, drawing curious glances and inquiries from passersby. He thrived on their reactions—the double takes, the impressed nods, the inevitable questions that allowed him to recount his success. He found ways to steer conversations toward his award, relishing every opportunity to mention the industry connections he had cultivated. Even casual outings became performances, each moment another chance to soak in admiration.

Abram and Sarra dismissed it all as harmless indulgence, but to me, it was something more—an insatiable hunger for validation and a growing detachment from reality.

By the time the Emmy Awards rolled around again the following year, I had hoped to share the experience with Adam. Instead, his response was dismissive: "I only watch the Emmy Awards when I've been nominated." It revealed so much about him—a man who valued accolades above all else, incapable of celebrating the success of anyone but himself.

Looking back, the signs were always there: the lies, manipulation, selfishness, and lack of empathy. Yet, I ignored them, excused them, and justified them because the truth was too painful to face. I wanted so much for our relationship to work, for the life we were building to be real. But the foundation was already crumbling, and I was too blinded by hope to see it.

Adjusting to life in New Jersey was far from easy. The colonial charm and academic ambiance felt like another world compared to the sprawling, laid-back energy of Los Angeles. While the township's picturesque streets exuded quiet sophistication, I found the environment stifling. It was as though the very air demanded restraint.

And then there was the commute from central New Jersey to Manhattan. It became both a necessity and a test of endurance. Each morning began with an hour-long train ride to Penn Station, followed by a brisk half-hour walk to my office near 42nd Street. On bad days, delays stretched my commute to over five hours round trip. Even with Franklin Ames Corporation covering my train tickets, the routine left me exhausted.

While the small university town we called home exuded quiet sophistication, Manhattan stood in stark contrast—loud, relentless, and overwhelming, a place where anonymity ruled and urgency colored every interaction. The streets pulsed with energy but also an undercurrent of danger. I avoided the subway whenever possible, its dark, grimy stations a stark contrast to the sunny streets of California. Yet, on days when bad weather forced me underground, I relied on the survival tips Robert had shared: Stay alert and never let your guard down. His guidance became a lifeline in navigating the city's intimidating landscape.

Work, however, provided me with a sense of pride and stability. My office near Grand Central Station buzzed with the high energy of Manhattan's corporate life. From my window, I could see the iconic spire of the Chrysler Building—a reminder of the city's grandiosity and my own resilience in adapting to it. Thriving in the fast-paced environment helped me maintain a semblance of identity amid the upheaval of my personal life.

Yet, looking back, those days in New Jersey—with their long commutes and emotional toll—were filled with signs that something in my life was off. Adam's frequent absences, his evasive moods, and my own sense of growing isolation should have signaled a deeper problem.

But my childhood had been shaped by uncertainty, training me to focus on endurance rather than reflection. I had learned to navigate hardship by pushing forward, relying on well-worn survival techniques rather than stepping back to examine my circumstances with clarity. There was no room for analysis, no energy left for questioning. I was operating on instinct, doing what I had always done—finding a way to get through. And in that relentless pursuit of stability, I failed to see the reality unraveling around me.

Two months after settling into university housing, Adam and I set out to find a bloodhound puppy, but our search came up empty. Adam had always wanted a beagle, and when we came across a tri-colored beagle puppy, we decided to bring her home. We named her Millie, and she became my lifeline during a period of increasing loneliness. As Adam traveled more often for seminars, guest speaker events, and consulting work, Millie filled the emotional void, offering the unconditional love and companionship I craved but didn't receive from him. Her boundless energy and affectionate nature brought warmth to a home that often felt cold and distant.

In October 1984, we welcomed a six-month-old bloodhound into our family. We named him Winston, fulfilling a childhood dream of mine. From the moment he arrived, he became part of our household, his soulful eyes and gentle nature filling our home with warmth and joy. Caring for him and Millie gave Adam and me a shared purpose—a rare thread of connection in our strained relationship. Weekends were spent walking them through town, brief respites that concealed the growing tension between us.

But our time with Winston was short. His health began to decline soon after he arrived, and despite consulting numerous veterinarians, his condition worsened. We celebrated his first birthday with cautious hope, but he had to be hospitalized the next day. A week later, he succumbed to an autoimmune disorder. Saying goodbye to him was one of the hardest moments of my life.

While I was consumed by grief, Adam's reaction was unemotional. Within days, he began contacting breeders, eager to bring home another bloodhound. His urgency to move on felt jarring, clashing with my need to mourn. A month later, we attended a local dog show where we met Samson, a five-month-old bloodhound. Despite my lingering sadness, I felt an instant connection with him and agreed to bring him home.

Samson brought a renewed sense of hope and comfort into my life. His goofy, endearing personality filled my days with genuine joy, and his bond with Millie helped soften the ache of losing Winston. Yet, Winston's passing also exposed the growing emotional distance between Adam and me. While I needed time to grieve, Adam compartmentalized his emotions, leaving me secluded.

I took solace in Millie and Samson, whose loyalty and love anchored me during a time of profound uncertainty. But beneath the surface, I couldn't shake the growing unease that Adam's charm and intelligence masked something darker—something that left me feeling unsettled and alone.

Balancing the responsibilities of a full-time job with the care of our two dogs was no small task for me. Yet, on weekends, Adam and I escaped into a world of dog shows across the Mid-Atlantic states. Samson excelled in the ring, captivating judges with his outstanding breed conformation and vibrant, playful personality. With affection, the judges nicknamed him the "flat-foot floogie" as they awarded him points toward his American championship.

It was at one of these shows that we first considered offering a retirement home to a five-year-old black-and-tan bloodhound named Lily. A seasoned show dog, Lily had earned the prestigious titles of American and Canadian Champion—clear proof of her exceptional conformation and showmanship.

From the moment I met her, I knew Lily was meant to be part of my life. I couldn't explain it—not even to myself—but the feeling was undeniable. If we didn't take her home that day, I knew the chance would be gone forever. Adam was taken aback by my uncharacteristic insistence, but I spoke from a place deep within—my intuition—and he eventually agreed.

Lily had presence. She was a natural leader, sharp-witted and self-assured, quickly establishing herself as the alpha of the household. Samson and Millie never stood a chance against her cunning. A perfect example: Whenever they were given new chew toys, Lily would wait a few moments, then suddenly leap up and race into the living room, howling at the large front window. Samson and Millie, ever gullible, would abandon their toys to investigate the imagined commotion. The moment they left, Lily would double back and claim all the chew toys for herself. By the time her housemates returned—confused and empty-pawed—Lily was already enjoying the spoils of her clever ruse. And they fell for it every time, much to her delight.

Beyond her brilliance, Lily had a remarkable sensitivity. She seemed to know exactly when I needed comfort, grounding me with her steady presence. Whether it was the weight of her head on my lap after a hard day or the way she'd quietly position herself between me and the world—as if to shield me—she filled a space in my heart I hadn't realized was empty. In Lily, I found an unspoken connection—a quiet, steadfast love that brought me a sense of safety, understanding, and belonging.

Evenings became a familiar rhythm. After work, I'd rush home to prepare dinner for Adam before he retreated to the basement for his woodworking projects. My time was spent with the dogs, grooming and caring for them in the upstairs bathroom. I loved brushing their coats, feeling the connection that deep care and trust can bring. Adam handled the financial responsibilities— food and vet bills—but the daily care of Lily, Samson, and Millie was mine. They were my children in every way that mattered.

Despite having three dogs, visitors always mentioned how spotless our home was. I poured myself into maintaining the house, proud of its warmth and cleanliness, though I never admitted that Adam contributed nothing to these efforts. His mother had always cooked and cleaned for him, and now that role had fallen to me. I didn't mind at the time—I was so happy to have a house, a home, and my beloved dogs. The work was exhausting, but it felt worth it.

In hindsight, I see how much of myself I gave away, blinded by the control Adam exerted over me. My joy in our home and our dogs masked the growing imbalance in our relationship.

On my birthday in 1984, Adam presented me with a beautiful diamond engagement ring. Overwhelmed with emotion, my first call was to Aunt Dorothy and Uncle Henry, who celebrated the news with a mix of joy and playful teasing: "After six years, it's about time!" Yet, our next call to Adam's parents brought a stark different response. Their lukewarm congratulations carried an undercurrent of disapproval. Despite converting to Reform Judaism before leaving Los Angeles, I remained an outsider in their Orthodox eyes. Adam reassured me that they liked me, but their quiet judgment lingered like a shadow over our relationship.

The following year, in November 1985, we purchased our first home—a two-story colonial near the university. With four bedrooms, two and a half baths, and a corner half-acre lot, it was the symbol of stability I had yearned for since childhood. Yet, as we signed the papers, a sense of foreboding gripped me. Though my name was on the deed, the echoes of my father's unfulfilled dream of owning a home on the marina lingered, turning what should have been a joyous milestone into a moment of doubt.

At first, I tried to dismiss the unease as simple nerves, the kind that come with making such a significant commitment. But the feeling didn't pass. It settled deep in my bones, a whisper of warning I couldn't ignore. I confided in friends, hoping for reassurance, but they brushed my concerns aside. "Everyone feels this way when making a big purchase," they assured me. "It's just the weight of responsibility sinking in."

But I knew better. This was different.

Adam, ever pragmatic, saw the house as a smart financial move, a way to build equity instead of throwing money away on rent. To him, it was an investment—numbers on a spreadsheet, an asset to appreciate over time. He had no emotional attachment to it, no deep-seated longing for a place to belong. When I voiced my fears, he dismissed them with a shrug. "It's just cold feet," he said. "You'll get over it."

But I didn't get over it. The house should have been everything I wanted—everything I had dreamed of since I was a child longing for permanence, for a place to plant roots. Instead, I felt like I was standing on borrowed ground.

I told myself to be grateful, to push aside the gnawing insecurity. After all, this was the moment I had worked so hard for.

And yet, a shadow loomed over it.

Looking back, I understand now what my intuition was trying to tell me. The house had never truly been ours—not in the way I had needed it to be. To Adam, it was bricks and mortar, a means to an end. To me, it was supposed to be home. But no matter how much I tried to convince myself otherwise, I couldn't shake the feeling that I was never meant to keep it.

I was right.

We moved in on January 25, 1986, marking what should have been the start of a hopeful new chapter. But three days later, the Challenger disaster shook the nation's collective spirit. While I grieved alongside millions, Adam's reaction unsettled me. He dismissed the tragedy with cold detachment, calling it a publicity stunt gone wrong. Beneath his criticism, I sensed a bitterness rooted in his unfulfilled dream of becoming an Air Force test pilot. His lack of empathy for the loss of life was a chilling reminder of the emotional gulf between us.

Looking back, the explosion of the Challenger was a forewarning of the personal and emotional explosion that would come later in my relationship with Adam. Just as the shuttle broke apart under forces too great to withstand, my own world would shatter under the strain of deception, manipulation, and control. The warning signs were there, but like so many watching that launch, I wanted to believe in the promise of what was ahead, unaware of the destruction that lay in wait.

Around this time, I transitioned to a management role at a multinational investment bank in Lower Manhattan. Encouraged by my mentor, Robert Katz, I accepted the position, drawn by its promise of growth. The increased pay allowed Adam and me to secure a favorable mortgage through the university, but the demanding commute and grueling hours left me exhausted.

At home, Adam's passions for woodworking and technology took center stage. His workshop buzzed with activity as he crafted stunning furniture. The basement became a gallery of exotic woods: black walnut, bird's-eye maple, zebrawood, ebony, and teak. Adam's creations—a display cabinet, dresser, and custom bookshelves—were beautiful. Yet, the late-night projects, constant sawdust, and fire hazards added tension to an already fragile dynamic. One terrifying afternoon, oily rags in the workshop spontaneously combusted, sparking a fire. I rescued our beloved dogs, Millie, Samson, and

Lily, and realized the burden of safeguarding our home rested squarely on my shoulders.

Adam's pursuit of status revealed itself in flamboyant ways. Obsessed with *Top Gun* and dressing like a modern-day cowboy, he seemed determined to craft an identity lifted from the silver screen—part Maverick, part Indiana Jones. His collection of exotic western boots, made from snake, eel, stingray, cowhide, lizard, alligator, sharkskin, and ostrich, was both extravagant and disturbing. He wore them with pride, oblivious—or indifferent—to the lives taken for his display of vanity.

His disregard for wildlife stood in sharp contrast to my passion for animals. Where I felt a quiet reverence for living beings, he flaunted their remains as status symbols.

Adam spared no expense on appearances. He poured money into elaborate landscaping, including a koi pond stocked with over a hundred fish, and filled our home with Tiffany fine china and Baccarat stemware. On the surface, we looked like the embodiment of success. But behind closed doors, our relationship felt increasingly hollow. The home, though meticulously styled, was never a sanctuary—it was a stage for Adam's ambitions, not a reflection of shared life or love.

The koi pond became my escape. While Adam's interest in it waned, I devoted myself to caring for the fish, learning their traits, and even hand-feeding them. Naming them brought me joy: Mura, with her mirror-like scales; Cruiser, the vibrant yellow speedster; and Ursula, the majestic three-foot German koi. The pond and its aquatic life became a source of peace, a stark contrast to the growing discord in my relationship with Adam.

By the early 1990s, the cracks in our relationship were undeniable. Adam's frequent absences and fixation on appearances left me isolated. While he hosted formal dinners to showcase his woodworking and entertained his colleagues, I remained tethered to our home's upkeep. Caring for our dogs, pond, and menagerie of animals filled my days, leaving little time to nurture my own identity.

The house, once a dream of stability, had become a velvet trap. Surrounded by material comforts and my beloved animals, I began to confront the uncomfortable truth: I had built my life around Adam's ambitions, but in doing so, I had lost sight of my own.

Sunday, May 22, 1988, dawned as one of those perfect spring mornings where the air was crisp, the sun warm, and the world felt alive. Like every other morning, I rose early, eager to start the day. I loved the stillness of those hours, the soft rustling of leaves and the gentle rhythm of the dogs stirring as I opened the back door to let them out. Millie, Samson, and Lily greeted me with their usual excitement. I exercised them, fed them, and checked on the fish in the pond, all while Adam slept upstairs.

After the dogs had eaten and returned to their beds, I hurried to prepare breakfast. By the time Adam emerged at his usual hour of nine, the kitchen was filled with the smell of coffee and toast. We ate together, lingering over the *Trenton Times* and *The New York Times*, savoring the unhurried pace of the weekend. Adam mentioned wanting to see a movie, and while he busied himself with the listings, I began tidying the kitchen.

I stayed quiet as I worked near Lily's bed. She was curled up, her black-and-tan coat rising and falling with what I assumed was the rhythm of her breath. She always loved her lazy mornings.

Adam eventually left to brush his teeth, returning as I finished the last of the dishes. The sound of his sudden, panicked shouting froze me in place. Adam was not one to show emotion, and his voice carried a terror I had never heard before. I rushed to where he stood by Lily's bed.

"She's gone," he said, his voice breaking.

I dropped to my knees beside her, placing my arms around her still-warm body. "Lily," I whispered, as though my voice alone could wake her. But she didn't stir. Her face was so peaceful, as if she were asleep, but the absence of her steady breath told me otherwise.

My heart shattered in that moment, but instinct took over. I ran for a blanket, and Adam helped me lift Lily onto it. We carefully carried her to the car, the weight of her body so familiar yet now unbearably final.

The twenty-five minute drive to the veterinary hospital felt like an eternity. Adam and I replayed every detail of the past twenty-four hours, searching with desperation for some explanation. She'd shown no signs of pain, no hint of illness. Nothing made sense. Tears streamed down my face as I questioned how such a vibrant, loving soul could be taken so suddenly. I had cared for her with every ounce of love I had, often putting her needs above my own. Why would God take her from me?

At the hospital, we told the doctors everything we could. They performed an autopsy, but it revealed no answers. Lily, they said, had the heart of an athlete. She was only six and a half years old—so young, so strong—far too full of life to be gone. Tissue samples were sent to several of the nation's top scientific labs, yet every report came back the same: inconclusive. Lily had slipped away without warning, leaving behind a silence no words could fill.

In the days that followed, fear crept into every corner of my life. I watched Millie and Samson constantly, panicking if they slept too long or if their breathing seemed too shallow. At night, as I lay in bed, I wondered if I would wake up in the morning—or if Adam would. My grief spiraled into a suffocating mix of depression and anxiety.

Desperate for relief, I sought therapy, joining a group session that met for several weeks. But the surface-level discussions left me feeling hollow, as though no one understood the depth of my loss. One afternoon, as I shared my grief over losing my dog, a participant turned to me and asked, "Why can't you just go buy another dog?"

The question landed like a slap. My throat tightened, and I struggled to find words. How could I explain that Lily wasn't an object to be replaced but a soul I had loved? That grief wasn't about scarcity, easily remedied with a transaction, but about a bond that couldn't be replicated.

I sat in silence, the weight of my emotions pressing against my ribs, realizing this space wasn't where I would find the understanding I longed for. Lily had been my anchor, my confidante, a member of my family.

I couldn't escape the image of her peaceful face or the thought that, perhaps, she had been called to the Light on the other side. Her passing left me questioning everything—the fragility of life, the suddenness of loss, and the aching, unanswerable question of *why*.

Even now, I find myself reaching for her in quiet moments, listening for the sound of her paws on the floor, feeling her absence in the empty spaces she once filled. Lily was a piece of my heart, and losing her left an emptiness that nothing could ever replace.

Less than a year after losing Lily, a sliver of light pierced through our grief. We learned about an eight-month-old bloodhound puppy named Mabel. Born on Saint Patrick's Day, her name—of Latin origin—meant "lovable," and it felt like a sign. With her gentle eyes and boundless energy, we believed Mabel would be the perfect addition to our family—a joyful, affectionate companion for Millie and Samson, and a healing presence for us all.

When I first met Mabel, her exuberance was contagious. She had a happy, energetic nature that made it impossible not to smile in her presence. But there was one concern: Mabel had developed a slight limp in her left rear leg.

While the injury wasn't severe, we monitored her closely to prevent further strain. Without hesitation, I resolved to help Mabel heal.

Every day for three months, I massaged Mabel's leg several times each day, paying careful attention to her movement and diet. I ensured her meals were nutritious and portioned, keeping her weight in check to avoid added pressure on her leg. I balanced moderate exercise with plenty of rest, letting her build strength. After many weeks, the limp disappeared, and Mabel moved with ease.

Mabel, like Lily before her, became part of my heart and soul. Her boundless joy and flexibility after overcoming her early challenges reminded me of the beauty in new beginnings. She helped fill the void left by Lily, bringing a renewed sense of purpose to my days. Through Mabel, I found healing—for her and for myself.

Three years later, Sadie joined our family, completing our pack of three bloodhounds and one beagle. Each dog brought Adam and me tremendous joy, each with their own distinct personality. Sadie, the youngest of the bloodhounds, was three years younger than Mabel, but her age didn't stop her from assuming the role of alpha. Samson and Mabel were content to let her believe she was in charge, often yielding to her dominant nature.

Although we had a strict rule—no dogs on the furniture—Sadie had other ideas. She would race into the family room, leap onto the sectional sofa, and howl at the others if they dared to follow her lead. It was clear that Sadie didn't see herself as another dog—she believed she was something more. In her mind, she was management, and the rest of the pack were her staff.

Chapter 12

A Journey of Love and Letting Go

In 1988, Adam founded AMR Scientific Consulting, specializing in advanced materials research, failure analysis, and litigation support. I took on the role of Operations Manager, implementing streamlined systems, transitioning the company to digital records, and securing major contracts that fueled its growth. My contributions were significant, yet Adam retained sole control of the financial rewards, always framing the money as "ours" while ensuring I had little say in its use.

The high-performance, German-made sewing machine Adam gifted me for my thirty-eighth birthday was a state-of-the-art setup, a true luxury in the late 1980s. Priced at $4,000, it featured computerized stitch creation, the latest computer technology, and a digital stitch display—capabilities that were groundbreaking at the time but are commonplace today. The computerized stitch creator allowed for intricate and customized patterns, while the digital stitch display ensured precision with every seam.

At first, I was thrilled by the extravagant gift—but the strings attached became clear. Adam had lofty expectations, and to meet his exacting standards, I tapped into childhood memories of watching Nanny sew, supplementing them with instructional videos until I mastered the art of crafting intricate men's shirts. He knew I was accommodating, and it was rare that I resisted his escalating demands. The sewing machine, though luxurious, was another tool in his need for control.

Over time, my life began to revolve around adapting to Adam's high-end lifestyle. We lived like a married couple, but we weren't married. I was fully committed to him, yet he was never committed to me. Adam manipulated me into believing he was building a secure future for us, and I clung to that illusion—even as the burden of his expectations grew heavier.

I lost count of the number of times I asked him, "Adam, when are we going to get married?" His answer never changed. "Soon," he would say, always with a casual shrug, as if I were asking about the weather. At first, I believed him. Soon meant we were working toward it. Soon meant there was a plan, even if I couldn't see it. But soon never came.

When I pressed further, asking for an actual timeline, he would sigh, sometimes rolling his eyes as if I were being unreasonable. "A marriage license is a piece of paper," he'd say. "It doesn't mean anything. I love you, and that's more important than a marriage license."

At first, I tried to accept his logic. After all, wasn't love the foundation of marriage? But the more I thought about it, the more I realized his words were a convenient excuse. He had no problem playing the role of a devoted fiancé in front of his family, yet in private, he refused to make it real. "A piece of paper may not mean much to you," I wanted to say, "but it means something to me."

And what of his parents? I often wondered what they thought as the years went by. At thirty, maybe they reassured themselves with hopeful excuses: *"He's focused on his career. He'll settle down soon."* But at forty? Forty-five? Their friends must have started asking. The family gatherings—those curious glances, the subtle questions: *"Any news? Are they finally getting married?"*

They must have been embarrassed. Maybe even humiliated. Instead of grandchildren, they got dogs. Instead of a wedding, they got silence.

Did they question his intentions? Did they wonder if he ever meant to follow through? Or did they believe the performance too—swept up in the fiction he'd created for all of us?

The truth is, I'll never know exactly what they thought. One thing I do know for sure—I remember what I thought.

"This isn't love," I whispered to myself one night, alone in bed while he was out of town again. "This is waiting. And I've been waiting long enough."

Adam's promises of marriage were nothing more than illusions— carefully crafted lies dangled in front of me to keep me tethered to him. His need for control extended far beyond the confines of our relationship; it spilled into every aspect of our lives, even the most public ones. At faculty dinners and university social events, guests could sense the strain between us—an undercurrent of unease that didn't require words. While his colleagues arrived with spouses and spoke easily of their children, Adam remained conspicuously unattached, still clutching the freedoms of bachelorhood. It didn't go unnoticed. His unwillingness to commit stood in stark contrast to the quiet expectations of the university, where family and stability were the unspoken norms. In that world, Adam didn't appear independent or unconventional—he simply didn't fit.

His dismissive attitude toward others became most evident during visits from Abram and Sarra. Adam made little effort to respect their strict Orthodox dietary traditions, brushing aside beliefs they held dear. They only visited twice during the twenty-five years we lived in New Jersey, but each time, I saw reflections of my own struggles in Sarra's subdued demeanor—the quiet signals of emotional abuse etched into the fabric of their strained marriage. I felt a deep compassion for her, recognizing that while our circumstances differed, they shared the same thread of imbalance and control.

As I reflected on our years together, the imbalance in our partnership became undeniable. Adam's selective commitment, his control over finances, and his preoccupation with appearances revealed the hollow foundation of our relationship. Despite my tireless efforts to build a life together, I realized that his true priorities lay elsewhere. The illusion of luxury and stability masked a deeper truth: I was living in a world of his design, one that left little room for my own needs, dreams, and sense of self.

This realization, though painful, was a step toward reclaiming my own voice and agency. It became clear that to find genuine happiness and fulfillment, I would need to break free from the confines of a relationship built on control and illusion.

Aunt Dorothy passed away in October 1990, at the age of sixty-six, following surgery for a congenital heart condition. From her childhood onward, she faced numerous health challenges, enduring multiple surgeries that often left her tired. Yet, despite her hardships, Dorothy radiated warmth and love, embracing life with an infectious humor that lifted everyone around her.

The night before she passed, she made an unexpected phone call to me. Though breathless, her voice carried its familiar steadiness. "I'm fine," she said, her words wrapping around me like a loving embrace. I had no reason to doubt her, no reason to believe it would be our last conversation.

The next evening, the phone rang again. This time, it was Ken, Aunt

Dorothy's only child. His voice, thick with grief, carried the unthinkable—Dorothy was gone.

The shock crashed over me, stealing my breath. I sat frozen, the weight of her absence pressing into my chest. Seeking solace in movement, I grabbed my sneakers, clipped on the dogs' leashes, and stepped into the night.

The crisp air nipped my skin, as if the universe itself was trying to steady me. My dogs walked beside me, their silent presence anchoring me when everything inside me felt unmoored. Each step was an attempt to outrun the grief, each inhale a battle to keep from unraveling.

And then, the card arrived.

The morning after Dorothy's passing, as I struggled with the void she left behind, a Halloween card appeared in the mail. My hands trembled as I opened it, knowing she had sent it days before her surgery. Inside, in her unmistakable handwriting, were the words: *"Don't be afraid. Love, Dorothy."*

It was as if she had reached through time to touch me once more. A final whisper of love. A message that defied death itself.

Divine intervention? Fate? I don't know. But I do know this—she died, and then the card came. And in those moments, when grief felt insurmountable, I was reminded that love never leaves us. It lingers in the echoes of a voice, in ink on paper, in the quiet presence of those who walk beside us until we find our footing again.

Dorothy and I were kindred spirits. We looked alike—red-haired, tall, slender—and shared meticulous attention to detail in keeping our homes in order. While I leaned toward seriousness, Dorothy balanced me with her humor. Our deep conversations were a source of trust and joy, fostering a bond that felt more like a mother-daughter relationship than that of an aunt and niece.

When Uncle Henry retired, he and Aunt Dorothy settled in Florida—close to his relatives and surrounded by the warmth of enduring friendships. This new chapter of their lives brought comfort and fulfillment, transforming ordinary days into something meaningful. Florida became more than a place to live—it became a true home.

Dorothy's passing left an immense void, one that neither routine nor time could fill. Her letters, brimming with wit and warmth, had been a constant source of connection. Yet, the Halloween card she sent before her surgery became her final gift—a tangible reminder of the love and comfort she always provided.

Her influence remains woven into the fabric of my life. Her resilience in the face of adversity, her ability to find joy in the smallest moments, and her love continue to inspire me. Even now, I keep that Halloween card in a special place—a testament to the enduring power of love.

Aunt Dorothy was my anchor, the one person whose love I never had to question. From childhood, I ran into her arms, soaking in the warmth and tenderness I longed for but seldom received elsewhere. Unlike my mother, who met my expressions of love with silence, Aunt Dorothy always responded with an unhesitating "I love you." In every letter we exchanged, we reaffirmed our love for each other—a lifeline for a child starving for affection.

Her sudden passing was a turning point. Without her, I felt adrift. Still, even in death, she left behind a lesson: resilience.

Her life, shaped by struggles and sacrifice, was a testament to perseverance. I admired her strength but longed for a different path—one where I could achieve financial independence and security. But Adam's manipulations left me feeling vulnerable, making it difficult to break free. Losing Aunt Dorothy deepened that sense of instability. She had been my safe haven, and without her, I was forced to navigate life's challenges without the love and reassurance she had always provided.

Even so, her memory remains a source of strength, her voice echoing in the quiet moments, reminding me that love—true, unconditional love— never fades.

In January 1995, Adam and I received difficult news—our beloved bloodhound, Samson, had been diagnosed with benign hyperplasia. This condition involves an abnormal increase in the number of normal cells within a tissue or organ, leading to swelling or enlargement, though it is not cancerous. In Samson's case, it had caused his prostate to become enlarged. At ten years old, Samson was entering his twilight years, and his diagnosis marked the beginning of his physical decline. Samson was more than a pet; he was a central figure in our family, which included three bloodhounds— Samson, Mabel, and Sadie—and our beagle, Millie. With his dignified demeanor and affectionate nature, Samson had a way of commanding attention while offering quiet comfort to everyone around him.

As Samson aged, the signs of his declining health became evident. He began to lose his appetite, and his once-enthusiastic greetings turned into gentle tail wags. His movements grew slower, and at times he seemed disoriented, often getting lost in familiar surroundings. Despite these changes, Samson remained gentle and loving.

Over the following months, his health deteriorated due to kidney disease and severe prostate issues. Caring for him became a full-time commitment, involving medications, vet visits, and round-the-clock monitoring. Despite the physical and emotional toll, I was dedicated to providing him with love and comfort. Adam's financial support and the compassionate care of our veterinarians allowed us to give Samson the best possible quality of life in his final months.

Our other dogs seemed to understand the gravity of his condition. Mabel would often sit by his side, offering silent companionship. These moments of canine empathy reminded me of the unique bonds animals share and the unspoken understanding that transcends words.

By August, it became clear that Samson's body could no longer sustain him. He had grown frail, his once-muscular frame reduced by weight loss and digestive struggles. The difficult decision to euthanize him was made with heavy hearts but also with the knowledge that it was the kindest act we could offer.

The day before Adam was set to leave for a trip to Seattle, I found him folding clothes and placing them neatly into a suitcase. I stood in the doorway of our bedroom, watching for a moment before speaking.

"Adam," I said gently, my voice already catching with emotion, "Samson may not have more than a few days left. Maybe less."

He didn't look up, just kept folding. "He'll be alright."

I stepped closer. "If you go… you might not be here when it happens. You might miss saying goodbye."

He finally looked at me, but his expression was unreadable—calm, almost indifferent.

"Why do you always focus on death?" he said flatly.

I blinked, trying to hold back the swell of grief and frustration rising in my chest. "I know it's hard, but being here for him now—*this* is what matters."

Adam shrugged slightly, as if the weight of the moment slid off him. "I have to be in Seattle for a meeting."

I stared at him, searching for something—anything—that showed he felt the same pull, the same sorrow. But there was nothing. No sadness in his voice, no hesitation in his hands as he zipped the suitcase shut.

Adam lacked the emotion I felt so deeply.

On Samson's final day, I stayed by his side, whispering to him and stroking his head. As the veterinarian administered the injection, I envisioned him restored to his youthful vigor, running in an open place free of pain. It was a bittersweet farewell—serene yet tinged with the deep ache of loss.

And Adam was in Seattle but in every way that mattered, he wasn't there at all.

In the days that followed, I struggled to adjust to life without Samson. His absence was palpable—in the quiet spaces he once filled and the routines that had revolved around his care. Cleaning and organizing the house became my refuge, offering a sense of purpose as I grappled with the void he left behind.

Yet, as I mourned Samson, another wave of grief resurfaced—one I had buried long ago. Losing him brought me back to the loss of Chalay, my plush toy chimpanzee, who had been my constant companion during a time in my life when love felt uncertain and out of reach. Chalay was my comfort. I had been alone in my grief when he was gone, with no one to understand the depth of that loss.

Now, with Samson gone, I found myself again mourning not just an animal but a soul. Samson, like Chalay, was more than what the world might have seen on the surface. He was a spirit I loved—and one who loved me back with quiet loyalty and grace. The bond we shared was real and pure, rooted in trust and care.

In contrast, my relationship with Adam now stood out starkly. I had clung to the fantasy that he loved me, but his actions revealed a different truth. Adam did not love me. The connection I longed for with him had been one-sided, built on illusion rather than devotion.

Samson and Chalay, though very different beings, had something in common: They were both real in a way Adam never was. They offered me something Adam never could—authentic love, free from manipulation or conditions. Their presence in my life taught me true love. In their absence, I am left with more than grief—I am left with clarity.

For the rest of August, I felt unmoored without the constant demands of Samson's care. Tending to our other pets helped, but the lighter routine left too much time for reflection. My thoughts often drifted to Millie, thirteen; Mabel, six; and Sadie, three—each one a reminder of the fragility of time.

I ruminated over my stagnant relationship with Adam. After seventeen years together, we were still engaged. Every time I brought up marriage, his response was the same: "Soon." The silence that followed only deepened the ache.

His pattern of withholding affection echoed my mother's treatment of me as a child. She never told Sally and Paulie or me that she loved us. Instead, she remained absorbed in herself, leaving us starved for love and warmth. What had once been a symbol of hope—the engagement ring—now felt like a shackle. When people asked about our wedding plans, I was ashamed to admit I had no answer.

When Adam returned from Seattle, he searched for another bloodhound puppy. While the thought of a new dog was comforting to him, I wasn't ready so soon after losing Samson. Grief hung over me like a storm cloud.

Disregarding my hesitation, Adam planned a vacation for us before he began teaching his class at the university for the fall semester. I suggested San Francisco—a city that held deep personal significance for me—but Adam preferred an international destination instead. It was clear this trip wasn't about easing my grief; it was about moving forward on Adam's terms, as always.

My father's family came from England and Scotland, which sparked my interest in visiting those places. But mixed feelings tugged at me. The trip would separate me from my dogs for over a week, and I couldn't understand why Adam insisted on leaving so soon after Samson's death. When I suggested we compromise—choosing either San Francisco or England—Adam's response surprised me. He decided we'd visit both.

Arranging care for our pets was my responsibility. Our veterinarian had a boarding facility and offered 24/7 care at their hospital, complete with climate-controlled kennels and exercise areas. A kind neighbor agreed to feed our fish, while a veterinary technician offered to care for Ruby, our macaw, with house visits each day. I spent days creating detailed care instructions, stocking supplies, and handing over keys and security codes. While Adam covered the costs, every logistic detail fell to me.

The day before we left, we dropped off the dogs at the veterinary hospital. Although I trusted they would be well cared for, leaving them was gut-wrenching. It dredged up memories of being left with strangers during my father's hospitalization, a reminder of the loneliness and how often I was cast off to strangers that defined much of my childhood. When I tried to express my emotions, Adam cut me off with his usual refrain: "Why do you always talk about death?"

Adam's own past was scarred by hardship, but he refused to explore it—or any topic that might deepen our connection. These "off-limits" subjects—marriage, emotions, grief—were the very ones we should have confronted. His lack of empathy, though perhaps not malicious, felt like a symptom of his narcissism. It echoed his father's stoic demeanor, leaving me to navigate my feelings alone.

Before dawn, a limousine whisked us to Newark Airport for our first-class flight to San Francisco. Adam's United Airlines benefits allowed us to bypass lines and enjoy priority services. I had never flown first class before and wanted to savor the experience, but a creeping tension unsettled me.

After boarding, I mentioned my curiosity about hearing the pilot's communication with air traffic control. Adam asked the flight attendant if we could listen. When she declined in a polite, professional tone, he pushed back, insisting that passengers had the right to access. Adam's voice grew sharp, and I shrank into my seat, mortified. She returned with two headsets—whether to appease Adam or to defuse the tension, I couldn't be sure.

What triggered his aggression? Was this Adam being Adam? Whatever the reason, the moment was ruined. I feigned excitement to avoid further conflict, but unease settled deep within me. Looking back, his behavior was always about control.

Later, I thanked the flight attendant for her patience. Her weary smile stirred a familiar feeling—I had spent my childhood as a peacemaker, apologizing for my mother's behavior, soothing Sally's outbursts, and mending conflicts. It was a habit I hadn't outgrown.

In San Francisco, we stayed at an elegant Union Square hotel with a stunning view of the Golden Gate Bridge. The city's vibrant energy stirred memories of our 1978 trip. We spent the day shopping at Velora Textiles, a renowned four-story fabric emporium celebrated for its extraordinary selection of high-end textiles—luxurious silks, rich wools, intricate laces, and specialty prints. It was a true paradise for designers and sewing enthusiasts, with shelves stacked high with bolts of fabric in every imaginable color and texture.

As we wandered through the aisles, Adam was naturally drawn to the pinstripes, carefully selecting fabrics for the custom shirts he hoped I would sew. His style was undergoing a transformation. He was shifting away from his familiar western wear, embracing a more refined and commanding business aesthetic—not the collegiate preppy look but something far more elevated and intentional. He had started investing in tailored suits, bold art deco ties, and gleaming monogrammed cuff links that caught the light with every movement.

Yet, despite the sleek evolution of his wardrobe, one element remained unchanged: his western boots. Crafted from rugged animal hide, they stood in stark contrast to the clean lines and polished elegance of his suits—a defiant mismatch that seemed less a fashion faux pas and more a subtle declaration of identity, a quiet refusal to abandon his roots.

Riding the iconic cable cars to Fisherman's Wharf felt nostalgic but lacked true joy. Adam seemed lost in another world, making me wonder if he was enjoying the ride at all. The joy of revisiting our days in San Francisco flickered—brief, elusive, and fading too soon.

The next morning, we drove to Muir Woods. As sunlight filtered through the towering redwoods, casting golden beams across the forest floor, a profound stillness settled over me. While Adam busied himself with taking photos, I stood in quiet awe, feeling as though I had stepped through the gates of Heaven itself. In the sacred hush, surrounded by ancient giants, my soul felt cradled and connected to the eternal.

Our visit to San Francisco was fleeting—twenty-four hours later, we were boarding a plane to London. The ten-and-a-half-hour flight felt endless, made worse by loud and restless children in the cabin ahead of our seats. Fatigue settled deep in my bones as we crossed multiple time zones, my body protesting the relentless pace Adam set. My feet swelled from the hours of confinement, a physical testament to the exhaustion that came with chasing time across continents.

In London, Adam spared no expense. We stayed at The Ritz-Carlton, hired a private driver, and toured landmarks like Westminster Abbey and Buckingham Palace. We shopped at Harrods and sipped afternoon tea at The Ritz, indulging in finger sandwiches and scones. It was like stepping into a fairytale, yet I couldn't shake the shadow of my past. Trauma is never left behind; it follows, even into gilded rooms.

Adam's excessive habits often clashed with my practical nature, but I didn't grasp the deeper issue until much later. One evening, a woman's critical remark about the abundance of food he had ordered at dinner was embarrassing, her judgment echoed my own unease. His over-the-top gestures weren't indulgent; they were a means of control, disguised as generosity. This pattern became clearer during our Buckingham Palace tour when he bought me a porcelain Queen Elizabeth II commemorative pillbox—along with others for his university staff. At the time, it seemed thoughtful, but in therapy, I would come to understand it as yet another way he asserted dominance, ensuring gratitude and dependency under the guise of kindness.

Returning home, we reunited with our dogs. Though Mabel and Sadie greeted us with wagging tails, Millie kept her distance from Adam—a silent reprimand he couldn't ignore. Holding Millie close, I felt torn between the pleasures of the trip and the precious time lost with my dogs.

Back home, the grandeur of Buckingham Palace seemed irrelevant. What mattered was the home I had, despite its imperfections. Still, I couldn't ignore the parallels between my life and the media's portrayal of Princess Diana, whose struggles with isolation and unhappiness struck a chord. Her story resonated as a warning, reminding me of the loneliness that can exist even amid privilege.

A few weeks later, we joyfully welcomed Max, a curious and lovable six-month-old bloodhound, into our home. His calm and affectionate demeanor complemented the vibrant personalities of our other dogs. Though he could never replace Samson, his presence was a balm for my grief. Together, the unique quirks of Millie, Mabel, Sadie, and now Max, filled our home with bliss and love—a stark contrast to the emotional distance in my relationship with Adam.

Seven months after our trip to England, Adam suggested another vacation. With the university's spring semester ending in May, he planned a two-week break before resuming his consulting work. This time, we would revisit London and tour Scotland.

Leaving the dogs at the veterinary hospital was as difficult as before, and the arrangements for Ruby, our macaw, and the pond fish added to the stress. I looked forward to Scotland's serene landscapes but dreaded Adam's relentless travel style. For him, travel was a status symbol, a way to accumulate frequent flier miles and fuel his narratives of international adventures. I, on the other hand, yearned for a simpler experience—one rooted in connection and mindfulness.

On the flight, I brought *When Wolves Remember: The Secret Grief of Wild Hearts*, a popular title prominently displayed in the souvenir shops of the airport. The book reaffirmed what I already believed about animals' capacity for deep emotion. Adam's obsession with luxury travel emerged again as he insisted we stay awake upon arrival in London to "adjust" to the time zone.

Exhausted, I struggled to keep up with his pace as we checked into The Ritz, too drained to appreciate the lavish continental breakfast. While the setting was stunning, its indulgence reminded me of a hollowness I couldn't quite name.

Throughout our last few trips, I noticed how much Adam had begun to resemble his father. His growing weight, fueled by lavish meals and endless hotel stays, mirrored his father's indulgent lifestyle. However, I brushed aside my concerns, convincing myself they didn't matter. His frequent tales of international consulting hinted at a life beyond my understanding—one he never let me into.

Looking back now, I realize there were all sorts of signs that Adam neither honored our relationship nor respected me as a person. But I ignored my doubts and decided to make the best of our trip. Although uneasy, I wanted to learn more about the history of the area—that's what made me the happiest when we traveled.

Later, we made our way to Oxford University, where a private guide led us through its storied campus. As we strolled along Queen's Lane and beneath the iconic Bridge of Sighs, I felt the weight of centuries pressing in around me. Oxford's legacy—as the intellectual forebear of America's Ivy League—resonated deeply, echoing the profound and lasting influence my father had on shaping who I am.

Driving past thatched-roof cottages, I was reminded of Nanny's Churchill Red Scenic dinnerware—cherished relics of family meals in the 1950s. The sight stirred memories of her insistence on Edwardian-era manners—maintaining eye contact, engaging in polite conversation, and sitting up straight. Those lessons, rooted in grace and propriety, had shaped my early life, their influence lingering long after childhood.

In many ways, being in England felt like returning to the life I had before my father's illness.

Adam found a historic tavern for lunch, and while he ordered fish and chips, I chose a garden salad and hot tea, a nod to Nanny's prudence and her disapproval of alcohol except for holiday recipes. The warmth of the locals felt like a brief reprieve from Adam's critical energy.

The next morning, we flew to Edinburgh, greeted by the beautiful strains of Scottish bagpipes at the airport. I wanted to linger and soak in the moment, but Adam rushed to hail a taxi, his impatience cutting short my enjoyment. We checked into a hotel with a view of Edinburgh Castle, offering a rare and welcome moment of calm.

I loved exploring the castle grounds and Princes Street Gardens. I felt a connection to the city's timeless and quiet beauty, though Adam's hurried pace left little room for reflection.

During a visit to the Royal Botanic Gardens, I once again found solace in the serene seventy-acre expanse despite the overcast weather. Adam, however, grew distant and moody, walking far ahead on our return to the hotel. His silence was a familiar pattern, and I chose not to press him, knowing his irritation would escalate.

Renting a car, we ventured into Scotland's countryside. Adam enjoyed the Whisky Trail, touring distilleries of Glenlivet and Glenfiddich, though the pungent aroma of whiskey didn't appeal to me. The beauty of the Highlands, dotted with sheep and Highland cattle, was more captivating than the luxuries of the distilleries.

Our stop at John o' Groats felt anticlimactic, with dreary weather casting a shadow over the experience. Mallaig, on the other hand, charmed me with its cozy cafés and shops, while a ferry ride to the Isle of Skye offered stunning views of seabirds, seals, and dolphins. These glimpses of natural beauty reminded me how much I missed our dogs, whose uncomplicated love contrasted with Adam's mercurial moods.

Returning to Edinburgh, we flew back to London and then onward to New Jersey. A minor mishap on the flight—a cabinet of dishes crashed due to unsecured storage—startled everyone, myself included. The sound of shattering porcelain sent a jolt of panic through me. In hindsight, it felt like a premonition. Those broken dishes symbolized the inevitable collapse of my relationship with Adam. Unbeknownst to me, this trip would be our last together.

A week after we returned, Adam left for an extended summer consulting trip to Seattle. I resumed the solitary rhythm of managing the household, his absence amplifying my feelings of abandonment. Each time he left, I grappled with the void he created, my resentment growing like a shadow I couldn't escape.

Months later, as I was beginning to rebuild a sense of normalcy, I received an unexpected phone call. It was Sally. Two decades had passed since we'd last spoken. I welcomed the call with cautious curiosity, unsure of her reasons for reaching out.

At first, Sally sounded wonderful, her voice brimming with warmth and familiarity. But within minutes, a strange shift occurred. Her tone and laughter became erratic, and her personality seemed to morph before my ears. As she spoke of her young son, her voice adopted an accent—a British lilt that reminded me of her teenage fascination with England. Then, her tone regressed to that of a young girl, wistful and full of childish giggles. Moments later, she spoke again, this time with the deliberate cadence of an adult.

The abrupt changes were jarring, and a deep sadness settled over me. It was clear that something was wrong. Sally wasn't the sister I remembered from our childhood—her fractured personality felt like an echo of someone I once knew but could no longer reach.

Sally's infatuation with British rock bands like the Beatles had been a defining part of her adolescence. She had dreamed of living in London, often mimicking British accents to draw attention. I longed to share my recent travels to England and Scotland with her, but I held back, afraid it might reopen old wounds or highlight the distance between the lives we now led. Instead, I let her steer the conversation, which spiraled in unpredictable ways.

I worried about the cost of the long-distance call, knowing her financial struggles. I suggested we keep the conversation brief. But Sally pressed on, her disjointed stories tumbling out with no acknowledgment of my concern. My unease grew. I told her I needed to end the call, and though she promised we'd speak again soon, that day never came.

Sally had become a stranger. Whether it was mental illness, therapy treatments, or medications, something had changed her. The sister of my childhood was gone, replaced by someone I could not recognize. Hanging up the phone, I felt a heaviness that lingered for days. The call was a painful reminder of how time, distance, and circumstance can reshape even the closest of bonds, leaving us to mourn the people we've lost and the versions of them we carry in our memories.

Part V

Reclaiming My Life

Chapter 13

Shattered Illusions and Healing Steps

IN 1997, DURING a consulting trip, Adam met Gavin Lin, the President and CEO of Thanica Industries, a Thai manufacturing company specializing in sustainable kitchenware and home cooking appliances designed for modern, eco-conscious living. Their shared entrepreneurial drive sparked a friendship, which led to a meeting in Bangkok. While there, Adam was captivated by Thailand's dynamic culture and the vast, untapped business opportunities it offered.

Leveraging his connections with Gavin, Adam was introduced to the president of a major Thai bank—a man his own age whose family had royal ties. This connection proved invaluable, granting him access to an elite financial network and positioning him within the country's top business circles. Gavin, a few years older than Adam, was born in China and educated at a private research university in New York City. Despite their diverse backgrounds, the three men formed an immediate rapport—one that deepened Adam's conviction that Thailand was a land of boundless potential.

Everything Adam touched seemed to turn to gold. Time and again, I had watched him navigate uncharted waters with an almost supernatural ability to seize the right opportunity at the perfect moment. If anyone could transform an ambitious idea into a thriving empire, it was Adam.

Leaning back in his chair at the kitchen table, he flashed a confident grin, the kind that hinted at his hidden secrets. His energy was electric—like a man who had cracked the code to unlimited success.

"The kind of deals I'm making in Thailand," he said, his voice thrumming with excitement, "this is next-level and life-changing."

I raised an eyebrow, both intrigued and wary. "Really? What kind of deals are we talking about?"

Adam's eyes gleamed with excitement. "I've been working with some serious power players. Gavin connected me with top-tier business leaders—one of them is the president of a major Thai bank. His family has ties to royalty. Do you realize what that means?"

I nodded trying to absorb what he was saying. "That sounds… promising. But what does it mean for us?"

His grin widened as he sat back, exuding an effortless confidence. "It means we're set. For life. The deals I'm making will open financial doors beyond anything I ever imagined. Thailand is an economic goldmine, and I'm getting in at the right time."

I studied him, skeptical but drawn in. "You think this is *the* opportunity?"

Adam nodded, his certainty firm. "In a few years, money won't even be a concern for us. We'll have everything we could ever want."

And the way he said it—the way he carried himself—it was hard not to believe him.

Adam and Gavin's brainstorming sessions often revolved around innovative product ideas. One day, I received a package from one of Gavin's client companies that included an electric multi-cooker. As someone who had relied on kitchen appliances for decades, I saw opportunities to improve it. When I shared my ideas with Adam, he dismissed them, prioritizing other projects. Determined, I wrote down my suggestions anyway. Though Adam faxed them to Gavin without reviewing them, my ideas caught Gavin's attention. Less than two weeks later, he called to express interest and proposed creating a new multi-cooker based on my recommendations.

Within six months, Adam and Gavin developed a prototype of the enhanced multi-cooker and unveiled it at a trade show in Chicago. A leading American multinational specializing in energy-efficient appliances acquired the manufacturing rights, allowing Gavin's company to produce the multi-cookers under its brand. Distributed through major big-box retailers, the product quickly became a commercial success. This milestone paved the way for Gavin's team to reimagine and upgrade other kitchenware and home cooking appliances, breathing new life into existing designs and generating fresh revenue and growth opportunities.

To my surprise, Gavin and Adam approached me with an unexpected proposition: They wanted me to serve as president of their new company,

Auralis Technologies, LLC. I accepted, excited by the prospect of leading the company's operations. Recognizing inefficiencies, I took immediate steps to modernize its financial operations by implementing a computerized record-keeping system.

What I didn't realize at the time was that Adam's university teaching contract prohibited him from owning a business while serving as a faculty member. He was also limited in the number of consulting hours he could take on with outside companies. This restriction had never come up in our discussions, so I had no reason to question his involvement. I believed we were building something legitimate—something that would secure our future.

During a visit to the distribution center in Texas, Adam worked with Auralis's attorney to finalize patent details. While there, he introduced me—by phone—to key executives who praised my contributions to the multi-cooker's success. Over the next five years, as president of Auralis, I oversaw the launch of five additional products and solidified our reputation in the market.

Yet no matter how hard I worked or what I achieved, my accomplishments always existed in the shadows of Adam's academic triumphs. Whatever he did was always bigger, better, and far more profitable, at least in the eyes of those who mattered most to him. The spotlight followed him relentlessly. His parents lavished him with praise, celebrating every lecture, publication, and university accolade as if he alone held the key to greatness. Meanwhile, my own victories, hard-earned and quietly significant, were treated as mere footnotes in his grand narrative.

I often felt like a background character in my own life story. Never good enough, never smart enough, and certainly never worthy of the kind of love and admiration so freely given to him. Despite my leadership, my innovation, and the tangible growth I brought to Auralis, I struggled beneath the weight of invisibility. My success didn't seem to count—not next to Adam's. And with each passing year, the gap between recognition and silence grew more unbearable, feeding a hollow ache that whispered I would never be enough.

While Adam's professional life flourished, my personal life began to unravel. His fascination with Thailand grew into an obsession, pulling him further from home. His career pivoted from experimental quantum science to consumer product design, and his prolonged absences left me juggling the company, our household, and our dogs on my own. Despite managing bills, maintaining our home, and ensuring the company's smooth operations, the strain on our relationship deepened.

Adam insisted that his frequent trips were necessary, assuring me that he had to be away from home to secure our financial future. I believed him, trusting that his work in Thailand was about business. What I didn't know at the time was the unspoken reason many men were drawn to Thailand. Along with negotiating deals, Adam was reveling in the company of beautiful young women—a truth hidden from me while I fought to keep our home from falling apart.

Our house began to mirror our lives. Once a shared project, it had become a symbol of neglect—leaking pipes, cracked vinyl flooring in the kitchen, threadbare carpet, and an aging roof choked with debris-filled gutters. With every storm, water spilled down the walls, a silent witness to the slow decay of both our home and our relationship. The damage was more than structural; it reflected Adam's fading commitment to the life we'd built.

The repairs piled up, but nothing was ever done. Adam ignored the deterioration, and I was powerless to fix it. I didn't have the means. Our money was Adam's. We had no joint account, and though I managed the finances for Auralis, I had no access to funds for our home. It felt as if the house was collapsing inward—storm by storm—and I was expected to quietly endure it.

Adam seemed to be running—not just from me but from his university colleagues and even his parents. I didn't know what he was escaping, only that his absence—emotional, physical, and financial—was etched into every broken fixture and every spreading stain on the ceiling.

Yet, amid the disrepair, I found strength in my work. My passion for innovation remained firm, and I leaned on my ability to adapt—something I had mastered long ago. Once again, I summoned the resilience to move forward, determined not to let the crumbling foundation of my home dictate the course of my future.

When Adam returned from Thailand to resume teaching for the spring semester, our days together should have felt familiar. Yet, on an early morning in March 1998, my life took an unexpected turn. A dream altered my reality in ways I couldn't have anticipated.

In the dream, Adam stood before me, capturing photographs of a young Asian woman and her infant child. The three of them radiated happiness and pride, an image of a perfect family. Though I was present in the dream, Adam ignored me. I knew, without explanation, that the woman and child were his wife and baby. The dream was so vivid it felt more like a memory than a fabrication of my subconscious.

When I awoke around 5:30 a.m., the dream clung to me with unsettling clarity. I could recall every detail, but it was the feeling it left behind that disturbed me. Deep in my core, I *knew* it was true.

Beside me, Adam slept, oblivious to the emotional storm churning within me. Careful not to wake him, I slipped out of bed and took my dogs downstairs. As they wandered outside, I stood by the glass door of the family room, staring into the dim morning light. The weight of the dream pressed down on me, an unbearable certainty gnawing at my thoughts.

I had to know. I had to either verify or dismiss the possibility of the double life I had seen in my dream. It wasn't a lingering fear—it felt as though I had spent the past several hours in two places at once. One in my bed, the other in a foreign country where Adam's secret life unfolded before my eyes.

Adam had never mentioned having children. The closest he had come was his offhand, sarcastic remark about pregnant women being "knocked up"—a cold, dismissive comment that encapsulated his often detached and insensitive attitude toward women.

Yet in the dream, he was a devoted husband and father. The stark contrast between the man I knew and the man I saw in that vision disturbed me to my core.

I had to uncover the truth. Thailand was thousands of miles away, and I had no idea where to begin. But a plan formed as my gaze fell upon Adam's overstuffed black leather briefcase sitting by the glass door. Driven by a mix of courage and desperation, I opened it.

What I found shattered my already fragile sense of reality. The briefcase contained letters from women in Thailand, Seattle, and Washington, DC, all addressed to Adam's university office. How brazen of him to receive love letters at work! These were a few of the many locations he had fooled me into thinking he was traveling to for weeks and often months at a time—on business, leading seminars, or attending conferences. Alongside the letters were photographs he had taken with his new camera. These images told stories of Adam's double life. One woman loved cats—a stark contrast to the Adam I knew, who would never tolerate having a cat. Another set of photos showed him vacationing with a woman in a beachfront bungalow, swimming and snorkeling, activities he had always claimed to dislike. I had never even seen Adam wear swimming trunks.

Each discovery unraveled another thread of the man I thought I knew. I took several letters and photos, leaving the rest untouched to avoid arousing suspicion. My heart raced as I pieced together the reality of Adam's infidelity, not with one woman but with many.

Weeks earlier, Adam had shown me a video of his recent trip to Thailand with his students. A beautiful Thai woman acted as their private tour guide, and Adam's camera lingered on her far too long. When I questioned his focus on her, he snapped, accusing me of being critical of Thai people and their customs. This was his pattern: deflecting blame and turning the tables on me, as he had done in countless arguments before. Resistance felt futile, a lesson I had learned all too well during my years in foster care.

That morning, I went through the motions of normalcy—feeding and exercising the dogs—but inside, I felt as if my world had shattered beyond repair. When Adam woke around 8:00 a.m., I could not bring myself to look at him. I was supposed to meet my friend Mary at 10:00 a.m., but the thought of casual conversation felt distant, almost absurd.

As I applied makeup to mask my swollen eyes, anger surged through me. I couldn't hold back any longer. I turned to Adam and confronted him, demanding the truth—was he having affairs with other women?

His reaction was chilling. Arms crossed over his chest, he stood tall, exuding a quiet arrogance. Then, with an unnerving sense of pride, he admitted it—yes, he had been unfaithful. But in his mind, the real issue with having multiple wives was the expense.

The audacity of it left me reeling. He believed I would sympathize with his financial dilemma, as if betrayal could be justified by a price tag.

Then came the final blow. "Look at yourself. You need to get checked out by a doctor," Adam said, his voice laced with condescension. He accused me of having a mental illness, likening me to my mother and Sally, even suggesting I was going through menopause. His words cut deeper than the betrayal itself. They were meant to destroy me.

Unable to endure his callousness, I retreated to my bathroom, locking the door behind me. I sobbed, feeling as though my sanity was slipping away. For two decades, Adam had been my rock, but now he was unrecognizable. I couldn't understand what I had done to deserve this betrayal. My self-doubt spiraled: Was I not smart enough? Pretty enough? Worthy enough?

Adam knocked on the bathroom door, his voice flat and emotionless. "Are you planning to commit suicide?"

There was no concern in his tone, no trace of worry. He wasn't afraid for *me*; he was afraid of the inconvenience. The last thing he wanted was to deal with the fallout. His question wasn't an act of care—it was a cold, calculating, and self-serving verification.

I refused to answer. I wouldn't give him that satisfaction. His arrogance was staggering—the sheer audacity to believe he was so indispensable that I would end my life over *him*. His emotional abuse had left me untethered, stripped of stability, but I would not let him define my breaking point.

By 9:30 a.m., Adam left for the university, leaving me alone in my despair. When Mary arrived, I poured out the morning's events to her. Understanding the seriousness of the situation, she encouraged me to seek professional help and recommended a nearby psychologist, Dr. Rachel Harris. Through my tears, I managed to call Dr. Harris and leave a message. To my surprise, she returned my call within the hour and agreed to see me around noon.

Driving to her home office felt surreal, as if I were caught between two worlds. Dr. Harris and her cat greeted me upon arrival. The cat, with a lush, long silver-white coat and eyes like pale sapphires—cool, clear, and watchful—offered an unexpected sense of comfort. During our session, I spilled my heart out. The cat sat quietly on the floor next to me, a silent witness to my unraveling. Dr. Harris listened without judgment, and for the first time in what felt like forever, I didn't feel alone.

The hour passed fast, leaving me with a mix of clarity and confusion. As I drove home, I questioned whether my experiences were real or imagined. One thing was certain: My old life was over. The daunting task of rebuilding lay ahead, and I would need every ounce of strength and support to navigate the path forward. Little did I know it would take years of therapy with Dr. Harris to unravel the depth of Adam's manipulations and the vulnerabilities that had made me an easy target for his control.

Later, I forced myself to focus on visiting my gynecologist for an AIDS blood test—an act of self-care to ground me in reality. Unable to bear the thought of sharing the master bedroom with Adam—or even being upstairs alone with him—I removed all my belongings and stored them in an extra guest room. At night, I didn't sleep there. Instead, I curled up on a tiny sofa in the living room, choosing proximity to the doorway exits in case Adam became violent. There, surrounded by the loyalty of my bloodhounds and my beagle, I found a semblance of peace and solace.

In the days that followed, Adam's attempts at affection felt grotesque.

His sudden proposal of marriage infuriated me. After years of yearning for his commitment, the gesture now felt hollow and manipulative. Rage overtook me, and I shouted at the top of my voice, "I will never marry you!" The intensity of my anger was unlike anything I had ever experienced. But within that fury was a spark of something new: determination. I resolved to rebuild my life, piece by piece, despite the wreckage Adam had left behind.

For years, Adam had claimed me as his spouse, insisting our common-law marriage was binding, even though New Jersey didn't recognize it. Yet, he never acknowledged our relationship to his parents, keeping me hidden as though I were unworthy of their approval. Looking back, I saw how vulnerable I had been when we first met in California. Alone and isolated, I mistook his intelligence and control for love, clinging to him in my desperate longing for stability and affection.

But now, as I stood amid the ruins of our relationship, I saw the truth. My worth was not defined by Adam's validation—or his rejection. I resolved to reclaim my life, to rediscover the woman I had always been beneath the layers of betrayal and heartbreak.

At night, I slept on the living room couch, a fragile refuge and the only space where I felt even a sliver of safety—my way of distancing myself from Adam. The isolation was crushing, but I wasn't entirely alone. I had confided in my neighbors across the street, kind-hearted souls who listened without judgment as I opened up about the fear and chaos in my home. Their compassion was a lifeline. They told me I could come to them anytime—day or night—if I ever needed to escape. "Just ring the doorbell," they said, "or knock on our bedroom window. We'll let you in." Their words offered more than shelter—they gave me a sense of dignity, reminding me that I mattered, that someone cared. When my AIDS test came back negative, I felt a flicker of relief, but the shadow of his betrayal lingered.

Adam refused to attend therapy sessions, dismissing my pain and belittling the entire process as pointless. He insisted that I was the problem. At first, his words were offensive—sharp and unforgiving—and over time, they began to echo inside me. I questioned myself constantly: Was I too emotional? Too demanding? Was this menopause? I didn't know what was real anymore, only that I hurt and that he didn't seem to care. Still, if I *was* the problem, then I had to find a way to fix it. I clung to that belief, not because I accepted his blame, but because it gave me a sense of control. Healing became my quiet rebellion, my desperate attempt to make sense of the madness. I didn't want to stay broken. I wanted to feel whole—even if I had to get there without him.

Dr. Harris asked me one day, "Do you want to stay with Adam?" Her question lingered in the air, heavy with implications. I hesitated, unable to imagine leaving, even as my love for him faded. "Leaving will be the hardest choice you'll ever make," she warned, her words both terrifying and true.

In the surreal weeks that followed, conversations with Adam felt like speaking into a void. His responses were cold and disconnected, as though we existed in separate realities. I tried to express my hurt, but he dismissed it, accusing me of being the one who had changed. He wasn't wrong—learning of his affairs had altered me. Therapy with Dr. Harris stripped away my illusions, revealing Adam's arrogance as a mask for his deep insecurities and his controlling nature as the foundation of our relationship. The revelations were both shattering and clarifying.

I met with attorneys to discuss a potential palimony case, but the legal jargon overwhelmed me. Each consultation felt like an uphill battle; my exhaustion and despair clouded my ability to process their advice. Frustrated attorneys grew impatient, but I felt like a desperate child lost in a fog. Dr. Harris encouraged me to take small, manageable steps to begin untangling my emotions. In doing so, I came to realize that I had been in love with the idea of Adam—not the man himself.

As the weeks turned into months, the Clinton-Lewinsky scandal saturated the media. The parallels to my own life were impossible to ignore— and impossible to stomach. Adam dismissed the controversy with chilling indifference, sneering at Hillary's appearance as though a woman's looks could somehow justify betrayal. He took it even further, arrogantly claiming that affairs were trivial in other countries, and that only Americans made a fuss over such things. The deflection was as offensive as it was revealing. His hypocrisy dripped from every word, a mirror of his own deceit. I brought these disturbing parallels to Dr. Harris, searching for clarity in the chaos. Both Adam and Bill Clinton operated like seasoned manipulators, twisting stories to dodge accountability and tighten their grip on control.

By September, my world crumbled further with the loss of Millie, my loyal beagle of fifteen years. She had been my emotional lifeline, offering unconditional love in a life filled with instability. Her passing devastated me, and Adam's indifference deepened my grief.

When I took Millie to the vet for her final moments, Adam refused to come. I couldn't help but wonder—was it because Millie had ignored him after our trips to England and Scotland a few years before? Had her quiet rejection bruised his ego so much that he would rather let me face this alone than offer even a shred of support? I held her close, whispering my promise of eternal love, as I mourned losing the one being who had never let me down—while the one who should have been there made his absence a final act of cruelty.

Although I had moments of profound sorrow, I began to understand the depths of my own strength. The road ahead was uncertain. I resolved to honor Millie's loyalty by finding a way to offer that same devotion to myself.

But just as I was learning to navigate that new, empty space, another heartbreak came barreling toward me.

Six months after losing Millie, Mabel—our joyful, rambunctious bloodhound—was diagnosed with liver cancer. Mabel had always been the life of the pack, a born entertainer who turned every walk, every car ride, every idle moment into an opportunity for play. I took her to the vet, thinking she had developed a skin allergy, but after bloodwork and diagnostic imaging, the doctors gently delivered the crushing news: Mabel had advanced liver cancer. Surgery confirmed the worst—nearly 90 percent of her liver was consumed by disease.

She was nearing her eleventh birthday. Her age, along with the progression of the cancer, led me to make the agonizing decision to decline a referral to a university veterinary hospital in Pennsylvania. The treatments would be too aggressive, and the travel too hard on her. I knew I had to let her go with peace and dignity.

The diagnosis hit me like a landslide. For several minutes, my mind went blank. Then I crumpled into tears. The veterinary staff—kind, familiar faces who had come to know not only Mabel but also the fragile scaffolding of my personal life—offered quiet comfort. They knew Adam was away again, this time on another extended trip to Asia, leaving me to carry the weight of yet another loss alone.

As the final injection was given, I held one of Mabel's front paws in my hand. I leaned in and whispered to her through sobs, promising her that I loved her and would always be with her in spirit. Nothing—not distance, not time, not even death—could separate us.

When I returned home, the silence was deafening. Sadie and Max, our other dogs, seemed to know Mabel would not be coming back. They sniffed around the house for her, ears alert, eyes wide with confusion. It took weeks for them to regain their usual energy. Like me, they sensed that something irreversible had shifted. Our once lively household now moved a little more slowly, a little more cautiously, as though we were all learning to live around an absence too large to name.

Depression consumed me. Adam's affairs, Millie's death, Mabel's cancer, and the looming loss of my home felt like an unbearable weight. The house, once my sanctuary, became a haunting reminder of everything slipping away.

At night, I would lie awake, staring at the ceiling in the living room, counting the cracks in the plaster as if they could somehow predict the moment when the walls would cave in around me. Each creak of the floorboards, each groan of the wind against the windows, felt like the house whispering its impending departure. The very place that had once held my dreams, my quiet moments of peace, now stood on the edge of becoming another casualty of Adam's neglect.

I felt utterly detached from all of humanity, as though I were floating in outer space—weightless, soundless—screaming for help that no one could hear. The silence was deafening. I was invisible, lost in a void where connection felt impossible and hope, unreachable. In that unbearable isolation, one truth became clear: no one was coming to save me. If I was going to survive, I had to find the strength to save myself.

Adding to my anxiety, Adam's sporadic property tax payments left our finances in disarray, turning my existence into a delicate balancing act—one wrong step and everything would come crashing down. He often dismissed the urgency, claiming that property taxes in New Jersey were too expensive, as if that somehow justified his negligence. His indifference toward the house was palpable; he treated it not as a home but as a burden to which he was tethered. Every month, I braced myself for the possibility of an eviction notice taped to the front door—confirmation, at last, that the life I had built was no longer mine to hold.

In the spring of 1999, Adam's university class partnered with Thanica Industries on a project that culminated in a student trip to Thailand. Eager for another escape, he volunteered as a chaperone. Yet, as his own videos later revealed, his attention was less on the cultural landmarks and more on their flirtatious tour guide. The trip itself unraveled into chaos—students falling ill upon their return, Adam's reckless decisions along the way, and a flat tire at the airport caused by his negligence in maintaining his aging conversion van.

The group's journey began with a long-haul flight from Newark Airport in New Jersey to Taiwan, before continuing on to Thailand. During the layover, Adam led the students to a well-known restaurant that specialized in traditional snake cuisine. There, he urged them—some said pressured them—to handle live snakes kept in cramped cages. For many, the experience was unsettling, as they were pushed beyond their comfort zones in an unfamiliar environment under Adam's forceful encouragement.

Once in Thailand, the risks escalated. Adam brought the students to controversial tiger entertainment facilities, where tourists could come into direct contact with captive Bengal tigers. Despite international concern over the ethics and safety of such venues, students were encouraged to pose for photos and even touch the animals—actions that put them in direct physical danger.

Several students later reported to university officials that Adam's behavior had crossed a line, describing instances where he used intimidation and manipulation to pressure them into participating in hazardous activities. His actions were characterized not just as reckless but as coercive, creating an atmosphere where students felt they had little choice but to comply.

Following these revelations, the university launched a formal investigation. The findings concluded that Adam had placed students in unsafe and inappropriate situations, adding to an already growing list of complaints about his judgment and conduct. As a result, he was barred from leading future university-sponsored trips abroad.

Although Adam secured tenure in his late twenties, his career soon plateaued. While his colleagues climbed the academic ranks, taking on greater responsibilities, he remained an associate professor, doing the bare minimum to fulfill his teaching contract. His lack of professional growth reflected the strained relationships he maintained within the university—an isolation further deepened by the fallout from the Thailand trip. The university's decision to bar him from future excursions underscored his precarious standing at the university—one that, in many ways, mirrored my own.

From 1999 to 2002, Adam's obsession with international travel grew. He spent months traveling through Southeast Asia, Australia, and beyond, only to reappear when I least expected him. My attorneys warned that he might relocate, fueled by Adam's mention of foreign bank accounts and property investments in Thailand. The fear of being left alone to untangle the financial and emotional ruins haunted me each day.

Meanwhile, complaints about appliances Adam had designed for Auralis began flooding in. Curious, I tested one myself and found it also failed after a few uses. Confronting Adam, I was met with indifference, a stark reminder of how distant he had become. His transformation extended to his appearance—jet-black dyed hair and fabricated claims of Asian ancestry. Even his parents, ever devoted to their "Golden Boy," did not refute or even question his lies.

Under Dr. Harris's guidance, I began to reclaim my life. I destroyed the scrapbook I had curated since 1978, donated Adam's gifts to charity, and focused on rediscovering myself. Adam's halfhearted attempts to win me back—offering material comforts or lamenting his loneliness—rang hollow. For the first time, I trusted my strength and began to move forward on my terms.

September 11, 2001, began with hope. A voicemail from a nearby company invited me to interview for a new position—a potential fresh start, a chance to rebuild. Just hearing those words felt like a lifeline. But as I prepared to return the call, the morning descended into horror. I watched in disbelief as the World Trade Center Twin Towers collapsed, the images on the screen searing into my mind. The destruction outside echoed the unraveling I felt within. In that moment, the hope of something new was swallowed by the shock of what was lost—not just in the world but in me.

That week in therapy, I confessed to Dr. Harris how disconnected and empty I felt. The grief of the attacks stirred compassion for the victims' families and an unbearable awareness of my own isolation. I wasn't suicidal, but I wished I could trade places with someone lost in the tragedy, sparing them for their loved ones. Looking back, I now see this as a blatant reflection of how little I valued myself in those moments.

In the aftermath of 9/11, depression enveloped me. I walked each day for hours through my neighborhood, trying to release the fear, sadness, and distrust that consumed me. But no matter how far I went, I couldn't escape the parallels between my life and the national tragedy—both marked by devastation caused by misplaced trust and poor judgment.

As days turned into weeks, I came to realize that every small step forward was a testament to my resilience. The road to recovery was long, but occasional glimmers of hope reminded me that even in the darkest times, rebuilding was possible. Yet, those faint sparks of hope had begun to fade.

The promising interview with the local company never materialized. In the aftermath of 9/11, financial services, tourism, and retail—industries that might have offered me a job—were in turmoil. Each rejection or unanswered job application made the walls around me feel tighter. Without work, I had no means to leave Adam. Like so many women before me, I was trapped—not by love or loyalty but by economic necessity.

Then came another blow. A call from my attorney's office brought devastating news: The lead attorney handling my case had suffered a heart attack and would be unavailable for months. Meanwhile, his colleague—the one other person familiar with the intricacies of my legal battle—was preparing to go on maternity leave. It felt as if every pillar of support was crumbling beneath me.

As my fiftieth birthday approached, a new fear took hold—the specter of age discrimination in an already struggling job market. An uncertain future pressed down on me, filling me with anxiety and an overwhelming sense of helplessness.

Meanwhile, Adam carried on as though nothing had changed. His life revolved around teaching at the university and traveling to Southeast Asia. When he came home, it was to grab fresh clothes before vanishing again into the night. He returned as late as two or three in the morning, slamming doors and waking the dogs—and me—in the process. His disregard for my presence was palpable, rendering me invisible in my own home.

I had long since abandoned our bed, retreating to a small sofa in the living room—a meager refuge that offered little comfort. Even there, I couldn't escape his disruptions. On nights when his late-night arrivals shattered the silence, I would lace up my sneakers and set out for a walk, sometimes as early as 4:00 a.m. The quiet, sleeping neighborhood became my asylum, the stillness soothing my nerves. Yet no matter how far I walked, I couldn't silence the anxious thoughts that churned in my mind.

It felt as though my life had collapsed, reduced to rubble like the Twin Towers. Love, trust, and stability—the very foundations I had built my world upon—had been nothing more than a facade. And the dust had yet to settle. I couldn't see a clear way forward, but I also knew there was no going back. Each day was a struggle to reclaim even the smallest piece of myself from the rubble.

Yet, despite everything, one truth remained: I had survived the collapse.

That alone was something. Perhaps survival itself could be the foundation upon which I rebuilt a life that honored who I was, recognized my worth, and reflected what mattered to me.

Beginning therapy with Dr. Harris marked a profound turning point in my life. Under her guidance, I began to confront the deep wounds and unresolved traumas that had shaped me—many of which stemmed from my complex and painful relationship with my mother. Throughout my childhood, I yearned for her love and attention, but she was consumed by illnesses: anorexia, bulimia, and an addiction to prescription drugs. Her haunting behaviors, like eating meals and purging afterward, were patterns rooted in her family's troubled history.

By the time I reached college, my mother's life was defined by hospital stays. Kidney failure led to dialysis treatments, and her growing dependency on medication was disguised as medical necessity. My stepfather, Doug, bore the brunt of her manipulations, enduring decades of financial and emotional strain as she skillfully exploited doctors and insurance systems to sustain her treatments. Though she presented herself as a devoted wife and mother of eleven, the reality for my siblings and me was in stark contrast. To us, she was an absent figure—present in physical form but unreachable on an emotional level—leaving us to navigate life feeling neglected and disappointed.

When she passed away in 1991, I felt no grief. We hadn't spoken in over a decade or more, and my longing for her love had long since been displaced by admiration for my father. Bedridden and void of affection, she became a cautionary tale for me—a reminder of what I never wanted to become.

Dr. Harris helped me unpack these complex emotions, showing me how they influenced my self-perception and my relationship with Adam. She marveled at how I had built a life from scarcity, contrasting it with the abundance I observed in Adam's parents. Their garage shelves were lined with a stockpile of canned goods and packaged foods that felt excessive for the two of them—remnants of a mindset rooted in overabundance and a fear of shortage. Adam dismissed my observations as sentimental quirks, but they highlighted the financial and emotional insecurities that had shaped my worldview.

Through therapy, I began to draw parallels between Adam's behavior and his father's controlling tendencies. Small actions—like insisting I stay indoors under the guise of "calming the dogs"—were part of a larger pattern of manipulation, isolation, and control. Once we started having dogs, he used this excuse, framing it as a necessity when, in reality, it was another way to restrict my freedom.

Dr. Harris helped me identify the red flags I had ignored for years: Adam's superficial charm, his manipulative tendencies, and his obsession with maintaining a polished image. She described him as exhibiting psychopathic and narcissistic traits—a lack of empathy, an insatiable sense of entitlement, and a willingness to exploit others for personal gain.

Hearing these truths was both devastating and liberating. For years, I had clung to a fantasy of who Adam was, unwilling to face the reality. Dr. Harris helped me confront my fears of abandonment, rejection, and financial instability—fears that had made me susceptible to his manipulations.

In one session, Dr. Harris surprised me with a simple yet startling statement.

"You're a strong person," she said, her voice calm but certain.

I shook my head. "No, I'm not," I insisted. "Strong people don't feel like this. They don't spend sleepless nights walking off sadness. They don't cry until there's nothing left. They don't—" I hesitated, my voice catching. "They don't feel this broken."

Dr. Harris leaned forward. "Strength isn't about never feeling pain," she said. "It's about facing it. And that's what you're doing."

I scoffed. "I wish I knew what it felt like to be strong."

"It takes incredible strength to remove the blinders that you have accumulated throughout your life," she countered.

I let her words settle in the quiet space between us. I had never thought of it that way. Could it be true? Was there strength in enduring, in refusing to turn away?

As I reflected, I began to see the truth in her words. My refusal to escape into denial or distraction, my determination to face my pain head-on—these were acts of resilience. Therapy became the space where I learned to reclaim my strength, piece by piece.

Dr. Harris helped me untangle the complexities of my past and guided me forward with steady, practical steps. She connected me with a family law attorney who brought not only professional expertise but also a personal understanding of my situation—he had gone through his own palimony case. Despite my financial dependence on Adam, New Jersey law did not recognize our relationship as a legal marriage, leaving me exposed and unprotected.

This legal reality only intensified my sense of shame. Still, I couldn't bring myself to reveal Adam's true nature to his parents. The thought of shattering their carefully preserved image of their "Golden Boy" felt like a betrayal I wasn't yet ready to commit. In many ways, I was still protecting the mask he wore—shouldering the burden of keeping his facade intact.

Meanwhile, Adam crafted his own version of the truth. He told his parents he wanted to marry me, and that I had refused him—that I had said I would never marry him. It was a lie, but one that conveniently cast him as the heartbroken hero and me as the one who walked away.

Adam and I shared the deed and mortgage to our home, owned five cars, celebrated milestones together, and I was known as Adam's wife within our shared ownership and involvement with Auralis. To his closest friends, I was "his wife"—a title he assigned me as casually as one might label a piece of luggage. At first, I assumed it was a gesture of commitment, a sign that he wanted our partnership to be taken in a serious manner.

But the cracks in Adam's facade became apparent when I noticed a different story being told to his family. To them, I was his fiancée—close but not quite the same. When I pressed him about this inconsistency, his response was cool and calculated, cloaked in the kind of condescension that made me question my own perception. "A marriage certificate doesn't mean anything. It's a piece of paper," he'd say, dismissing my concerns with a wave of his hand. "Why do you care what anyone else thinks?"

Adam had a knack for spinning realities. He crafted different tales depending on who was listening, always careful to maintain control. If I protested, he'd shift the focus to my alleged insecurities or claim that I was being irrational. His ability to deflect and manipulate was as precise as a surgeon's scalpel, leaving me questioning my own judgment at every turn.

In private, Adam's behavior often felt like a staged performance, designed to serve his own needs. One day, he would shower me with affection; the next, he would withdraw it, keeping me on edge. He made me feel as though I was the one failing him. His charm was a double-edged sword—enough to pull me back in but sharp enough to wound when I got too close.

Adam's psychopathy revealed itself in the way he used my love for him as leverage. He knew how much I valued commitment and stability, and he wielded that knowledge like a weapon. The roles he cast me in—wife, fiancée, partner—were not reflections of who I was to him but tools to serve his agenda.

What I didn't realize then was that I wasn't living a shared life with Adam.

I was living inside the story he constructed, a plot where his needs, his image, and his control reigned supreme. By the time I saw through his manipulation, the lines between truth and illusion had blurred almost beyond recognition.

Memories of my confrontation with Eliza Wu in 1983 haunted me. Her blunt words cut deep. "Adam doesn't love you," she said. "The only reason he's with you in New Jersey is because I'm here in California finishing my degree." Her perspective upended everything I had clung to, but I had continued to believe Adam's reassurances, desperate to hold on to the life we were building.

It was Dr. Harris who began the painstaking work of helping me remove the blinders I had worn for so long. By then, trust didn't come easily to me. I had lost that sense of safety with Adam. But there was something about Dr. Harris's calm, steady presence that allowed me to exhale—just enough to begin.

Each session felt like peeling back a layer of wallpaper in an old house, one that had been redecorated to conceal the rot beneath. The damage wasn't obvious at first, but it was there. Hidden. At the beginning, I could only manage small revelations—the way Adam casually dismissed my concerns, his consistent pattern of emotional withdrawal. Little by little, those truths surfaced, and with them, the slow and painful unraveling of a narrative I had clung to for far too long.

But Dr. Harris pushed me to look deeper.

"Who is Adam, really?" she'd ask, her tone both curious and firm. It was a question I had avoided answering for years because the truth was too painful. The person I thought Adam was—the person I loved and admired— didn't exist. He was a curated image, a reflection of what he wanted others to see. With Dr. Harris's guidance, I began to see the inconsistencies, the manipulation, the lies I had ignored or rationalized away.

In one session, I spoke to Dr. Harris about Adam's travels, which had begun while he was still in college. After obtaining his pilot license, he worked for a company that flew executives to destinations throughout the eastern United States and Canada. His job as a pilot had even helped him earn money during the summer. As I explored this topic with Dr. Harris, I couldn't help but wonder—was this the beginning of his way of living a double life? Had he first learned to compartmentalize his identities during those years, slipping between personas as he traveled between cities?

I came to understand that Adam's charm wasn't genuine; it was a tool he used to disarm and control. The affection he showed me wasn't love; it was a transaction meant to keep me tethered to him. Piece by piece, Dr. Harris helped me dismantle the pedestal I had placed him on, replacing the distorted image of him with the stark reality.

The process was neither quick nor painless. There were days when the weight of it all felt unbearable, when I wondered if I had been complicit in my own undoing. But Dr. Harris was always there to remind me that seeing the truth was an act of courage, not failure.

By the time I walked away from Adam for good, I no longer felt like a character in his story. I was, for the first time in years, the author of my own life. The blinders were gone, and with them, the illusions that had kept me trapped. What remained was clarity, hard-won and liberating, and a resolve to never let anyone write my narrative for me again.

A nagging question arose many times in my mind, whether in therapy with Dr. Harris or during my morning speed walking exercise: What would my father think of me if he watched me as I struggled with my challenges? Would he still love me and be proud of me? Would he confide in me that he had been blinded in his marriage to my mother? Was he manipulated by my mother as I had been by Adam? Was I more like him than I thought? Hadn't Doug also been manipulated by my mother into getting married when they knew little of each other?

These lingering questions pushed me further in my journey of self-discovery, strengthening my resolve to break free from the cycles of manipulation and control that had defined so much of my life. With Dr. Harris's guidance, I began to believe in my own strength—and my ability to create a life that was my own.

Continuing my therapy session with Dr. Harris, I recounted another profound event that occurred in May 1988 when my bloodhound, Lily, passed away at the age of six and a half. Despite thorough postmortem examinations, the veterinarians could not determine the cause of her sudden death, deeming it unknown even after sending samples for testing to reputable institutions and laboratories.

Lily's unexpected demise traumatized me, and I found myself unable to cease the tears. In my grief-stricken state, two weeks after Lily's passing, she appeared to me in a dream. We found ourselves within the Light, in a space resembling a tunnel. The sheer joy of being reunited with her overwhelmed me. I embraced Lily, desperate to hold on to her. Without words, she conveyed to me that I could choose to join her. I explained that I couldn't follow her yet as I had unfinished work to accomplish on Earth. The next instant, I found myself back in my bed trembling and weeping. I had made the conscious choice to be here, but I yearned to be with Lily in the Light.

Dr. Harris listened, her expression gentle and empathetic. "Cynthia," she said, her voice soft and reassuring, "what you experienced is often described as a paranormal event. It's not uncommon for people who are connected to their loved ones—whether human or animal—to have such encounters. These moments can be transformative, offering both comfort and guidance in times of profound loss."

Her words were a revelation. I had always been cautious about discussing the paranormal events that had occurred throughout my life, fearing judgment or misdiagnosis. It had taken me eight years of therapy to feel safe enough to share these profound personal experiences with her. To my relief, Dr. Harris accepted them and validated their significance.

"I believe Lily came to you in a moment when you needed her most," she continued. "She offered you love and choice, showing you that even in her passing, her connection to you remains. These experiences, while extraordinary, are also meaningful. They can provide insights that conventional explanations cannot."

Her acceptance of my dream and acknowledgment of it as a paranormal experience allowed me to embrace it without fear or self-doubt. I also shared with her the experiences I had with Chalay, my toy chimpanzee, who had been a special guardian angel to me in my childhood. A plush toy that could communicate with me was a stretch by all means of imagination, yet Dr. Harris understood. With a thoughtful smile, she remarked, "You know, Cynthia, I am still learning."

Her words echoed in my heart. For the first time, I felt seen and heard—not as someone who needed to be "fixed" but as a person with a unique and profound connection to the spiritual realm. With Dr. Harris's guidance, I began to view these experiences not as anomalies to be hidden but as meaningful parts of my journey, enriching my understanding of life, loss, and love.

Chapter 14

New Horizons

IN MARCH 2003, the moving van arrived. I was fifty years old. With each box of personal belongings being loaded, it felt as though fragments of my old life were being packed away—ready to make space for something new. My destination was a modest apartment less than six miles away. Though small, it symbolized the sweeping changes reshaping my world.

Since 1998, I had searched for a job aligned with my passions, but every attempt ended in disappointment. The lack of professional fulfillment intensified the financial strain as I prepared to leave Adam. In therapy, I vented my frustrations to Dr. Harris, who shared my disillusionment with the legal system. My attorneys had failed to secure financial support, leaving me to navigate a steep uphill climb alone.

As I stood in the entrance doorway for the last time, poised to walk away from the life we had built, Adam spoke. His voice low with regret: "I must have had a moment of insanity. I'm sorry." The words hung in the air, heavy and unresolved. I couldn't respond. The ache in my chest was too raw, the pain too deep for words.

The agonizing part of leaving was saying goodbye to my two dear bloodhounds, Sadie and Max. They had been my comfort through years of turmoil—their soulful eyes and gentle presence a balm when I had no one else. They were my family, my children. Leaving the house was hard enough, but walking away from them was unbearable. Adam had the financial means to care for them as they aged, and I had to trust that he would.

From the moment I learned of Adam's affairs, I knew that losing them would be an inevitable consequence of my departure. That knowledge crushed me. It wasn't just about finding a place to live—every affordable rental came with a strict no-pets policy—it was also about what I could no longer provide. Their veterinary care was becoming more frequent, and deep down, I knew I couldn't give them what they needed.

In the days leading up to my departure, I savored every moment with them, whispering promises that my love would never fade, even if I could no longer be the one to care for them. I ran my hands over their wrinkled brows and traced the softness of their ears, trying to memorize every detail—knowing those memories would have to last a lifetime.

The final goodbye was devastating. I held them close, burying my face in their fur, breathing them in as if I could somehow preserve the scent of home and love they carried. Sadie leaned into me with her usual quiet understanding, the kind of gentle presence that had always comforted me more than words ever could. Max—ever sensitive to my emotions—pressed into my side, as if trying to hold me there just a little longer.

When it was time to go, I forced myself not to look back. If I had, I might never have found the strength to walk away. The ache of missing them has never faded—it lives in a quiet corner of my chest, where their love still lingers, soft and steady.

Seven months after I left, Sadie died of complications from old age. It was as if, with me gone, she had completed her last act of grace—holding on long enough to make sure I was safe, then slipping away quietly, as she had lived. I wept when I heard. There are no words to describe the hollow that formed inside me knowing she was gone. The stillness of that loss settled into my bones.

Max lived for nearly five more years, reaching almost eleven years of age—old for a bloodhound. He aged slowly, gracefully, his once boundless energy mellowing into a watchful calm. And even though I wasn't there, a part of me believes he felt my love across the distance.

My longtime neighbors and the veterinary technicians—who all knew about the complicated and painful circumstances surrounding Adam—kept me informed about both Sadie and Max. They assured me that Adam spared no expense for their care and comfort. For that, I am grateful. Despite everything else, Sadie and Max were given the finest medical care along with soft beds and kindness.

But no matter how much time has passed, I still carry them with me. In dreams. In silence. In every breath where memory still lingers like the scent of fur and sunlit mornings. They were my four-legged children—and that truth will never change.

Though I stood firm in my decision, doubt lingered. In therapy, I often wrestled with the question: Had I done the right thing by leaving Adam? I replayed every moment, every conversation, searching for clues—wondering if I had misread the signs or acted too hastily. Friends and neighbors, many of whom had faced similar betrayals, offered their reassurances: "You did the right thing. Move on with your life."

But their well-meaning words couldn't silence the deeper unease—the mistrust I carried toward others and within myself.

One woman dismissed my turmoil outright. Her words still echo.

"You should forget the whole situation," she said, her tone flat and unbothered. "Most men cheat on their wives—it's a way of life. Find something you like to do and forget it."

"Forget it?" I asked, trying to keep my voice steady. "How do you forget a betrayal that cracked open everything you thought was real?"

"You think you're the only one this has happened to?" she replied, eyes narrowing slightly. "We all go through it. You just learn to live with it. That's what marriage is—compromise, even when it hurts."

"That doesn't feel like compromise," I said quietly. "It feels like surrender."

She gave a dry laugh. "You think starting over is easy? You'll be scraping by. Struggling with bills. Regretting this choice every time you can't make rent. You'll miss the comfort, even if it came with pain."

I didn't answer. Her words—sharp, absolute—burrowed into my mind. A part of me wanted to reject them outright, but another part, the one haunted by uncertainty, absorbed every warning.

Her voice faded, but the doubt lingered. Was she right? Had I doomed myself to hardship over some foolish notion of dignity and self-respect? The questions followed me like a shadow, especially in the quiet moments—when the loneliness crept in, or the bills piled up, and I questioned whether I had been brave... or reckless.

Had I miscalculated? Had I traded one form of suffering for another? I had spent years deciphering Adam's moods, tiptoeing around his expectations, and questioning whether I was the problem. And now, even free from his grip, uncertainty followed me everywhere.

And then, unexpectedly, another woman reacted in a way I hadn't anticipated at all. After hearing what had happened with Adam, she shook her head and said, "I wish my husband would cheat on me. I wouldn't mind divorcing him, but knowing him, he'd never do that."

I stared at her, caught off guard—not just by her words but by the casual way she tossed them out, as if betrayal might be a gift. Her comment lingered with me, too, not because it offered comfort but because it revealed just how complex—and quietly desperate—some marriages are.

At the grocery store, I scrutinized every item on my receipt, convinced that I had been overcharged or that I had made a mistake in selecting the wrong brand or quality. I second-guessed the simplest choices, standing frozen in the aisle as I debated between two similar cartons of milk, fearing that one was the wrong one, though I couldn't articulate why.

When someone gave me directions, I had to verify them multiple times. Were they sure? Did they know? What if I got lost? What if they had told me wrong—not out of malice but because people were fallible?

Rebuilding a life at fifty with no guarantees left me feeling as though I were standing on a tightrope with no safety net beneath me. Every step felt tentative. Every decision loomed large. If I had been so wrong before—so blind to Adam's manipulations—how could I trust myself not to stumble into another disaster?

Doubt was more than an emotion—it was a constant presence, a shadow trailing my every choice, whispering that I was unprepared, unequipped, and perhaps even undeserving of something better. But instead of pushing it away, I listened. Over time, I learned to question doubt itself, to recognize when it was protecting me and when it was holding me back. I didn't silence that voice. Moving forward without looking back didn't happen all at once, but with each step, certainty took root where hesitation once lived.

I reminded myself that enduring Adam's infidelity, gaslighting, and manipulative, narcissistic behavior had chipped away at my sense of self. Yet, the prospect of facing the world alone felt as daunting. Insecurity and loneliness loomed like a shadow.

I knew there was no going back. With Dr. Harris's support, I resolved to confront my fears head-on. Loneliness, vagueness, and self-doubt would not define me. Step by step, I was determined to build a future that belonged to me—one not dictated by fear but by the quiet strength of reclaiming my own life.

From 2003 to late 2008, I searched for work, relying on credit card advances to make ends meet. Before Christmas in 2004, I landed a role at a pharmaceutical marketing firm, managing forty projects and multimillion-dollar budgets. I optimized operations and enhanced client satisfaction, but after six months, restructuring led to my layoff, leaving my finances strained once again.

By mid-2005, a former colleague invited me to a Toastmasters International meeting, where I delivered an impromptu speech about my father. As I spoke, memories of his compassion and courage poured out, raw and unfiltered. The room fell silent, absorbed in my words—until the final moment, when the audience rose in a standing ovation. I was awarded Best Table Topics Speaker that night, but more than the recognition, it was the realization that stayed with me: Authenticity had power. That moment became a turning point, revealing not that I could speak with passion in front of strangers but that my story mattered. Even then, I understood—this truth would carry me through uncertain times.

My spiritual experiences with the Light became a source of strength as I rebuilt my life. They reassured me that I was never alone. The boundless love and comfort I found in the Light guided me through doubt and pain, reinforcing my resilience and reminding me that my purpose extended beyond survival—I was meant to grow, to heal, and to help others do the same.

One encounter in particular affirmed this path. In the early hours of the morning, I awoke to find my bedroom bathed in white light. Unlike sunlight or electric bulbs, it cast no shadows. Looking toward my large double windows, I saw darkness outside. But within the Light, there was clarity and understanding. Words were unnecessary; everything was known, pure and absolute.

Drawn by love, I rose from my bed, merging with the Light. The walls of my apartment dissolved. My physical form no longer existed—I *was* Light. Time felt infinite, yet in that space, I understood I had a choice: to continue as a spiritual being or return to my earth existence. With no immediate obligations—no spouse, children, or responsibilities beyond my own survival—I chose to stay.

When I woke, the darkness had returned, but so had an overwhelming sense of peace. I felt loved, secure, and safe. I knew I had stepped beyond my human life, immersing myself in the Light—a respite before returning to my earth path.

These experiences were not new. Since childhood, I had transitioned in and out of the Light, embracing my true essence: pure Light from Light. Before my birth, I remembered being part of it. I resisted coming to Earth, yet I chose to descend. And time and time again, I have chosen to stay.

I am convinced that all living beings—people, plants, and animals—are intertwined within the Light, connected beyond what we perceive in this world.

It took seven months to secure employment again, this time as an operations and project management consultant for an international candy product development start-up. Founded by recent Ivy League graduates, the company buzzed with youthful energy—a sharp contrast to my own perspective. At fifty-four, I was old enough to be their mother, and at times, I felt every bit the outsider in a world moving at a pace and tone not entirely my own.

From day one, I made significant improvements across operations, project management, public relations, and client relations. I streamlined strategic planning, implemented customer service enhancements, resolved complaints, conducted audits, and monitored web-based orders, including fulfillment, returns, credits, and back orders. My efforts optimized efficiency and uncovered emerging customer trends.

In two months, I recovered over $100,000 in delinquent accounts. Drawing on my experience at Auralis, I also managed international logistics for five major food and beverage trade shows. This involved budgeting, ROI analysis, registration coordination, sales materials, advertising, booth shipment logistics, and travel arrangements for personnel. Collaborating with the Sales and Marketing Department, I ensured seamless execution.

I thrived in the fast-paced environment, enjoyed working with the executive team, and delivered measurable results. When financial constraints hit, the company could no longer sustain my role. My tenure lasted less than six months.

Once again, I found myself at a crossroads. Despite my expertise in optimizing operations, recovering lost revenue, and orchestrating global trade shows, I was back in the job market. It wasn't the first time—and I knew it wouldn't be the last. Still, I remained committed to leveraging my skills, building strong relationships, and finding innovative solutions. The challenges of the physical world persisted, but so did my resilience.

This was becoming a pattern: securing a job, making a meaningful impact, and then losing it after a few months. No matter how skilled or determined

I was, stability remained elusive. I pressed on, undeterred, but uncertainty was real. Resilience wasn't a choice; it was a necessity. Still, it was hard—navigating life on my own, picking up the pieces time and time again, and willing myself to believe that the next opportunity would last.

And then, in the spring of 2006, another profound spiritual experience reaffirmed my faith in the Light. During a visit with my friends Amelia and Julian, their son Jason arrived distraught. His friend Dylan had lost his wallet, which contained vital documents, and was spiraling into despair, expressing suicidal thoughts. A deep knowing settled over me—a spiritual calling I could not ignore. I asked Julian for a quiet space, and there I entered a meditative state, seeking guidance from the Divine Light.

In my vision, I saw the wallet—a brown, overstuffed object—on the floor at the head of a twin bed near a wall radiator. When I returned to the family and described its precise location, Amelia and Jason rushed to Dylan's student housing at the nearby university. To their astonishment, the wallet was where I had seen it. The relief and joy were overwhelming. Later, when I met Dylan, we embraced like old friends, bound by an unspoken spiritual connection.

This moment was yet another affirmation of the Light's power and the unseen threads that bind us all. In times of need, we are never alone. The Light had guided me through my darkest moments, and now, it was showing me that my path—however uncertain—was never without purpose.

Leaving New Jersey had been building for years—a quiet restlessness that began simmering when I arrived in 1983. The town had given me stability, a space for healing, but its ivy-covered walls and quiet, predictable rhythm had begun to feel like a gilded cage. I needed movement, change, and, most of all, distance—from memories and patterns that felt overwhelming.

My thoughts drifted back to Los Angeles—a city I loved and missed deeply. I longed for its sprawling highways, sun-drenched beaches, and the vibrant, frenetic energy that sharply contrasted with the Collegiate Gothic stillness and measured calm surrounding me. But it wasn't the change of scenery that drew me. LA offered something New Jersey never could: anonymity. Reinvention wasn't possible there—it was inevitable. More than anything, it posed a challenge: Could I step beyond the confines of who I had been?

Still, the decision wasn't easy. Dr. Harris, my anchor through years of self-discovery, was nearing retirement. Her calm presence had been my lighthouse through countless storms, and the thought of leaving her physical presence behind filled me with doubt. But, in true Dr. Harris fashion, she met my anxiety with a solution.

"We can continue our sessions by phone," she assured me one morning, her voice steady and warm. "Retirement doesn't mean I'll stop being here for you. It means I'll be here in a different way."

Her willingness to adapt to my leap westward solidified my resolve. If Dr. Harris, in the twilight of her career, could embrace change, why couldn't I? Our phone sessions became part of the plan—a tether to the stability I was leaving behind.

By September 2008, as the global economy spiraled into collapse, I faced my own unpredictability. Job prospects were ambiguous, but I refused to let that deter me. Dr. Harris was preparing for a transition of her own, setting out for a quiet island off the coast of the Northeast. It was time for mine. With or without a job, I was going to LA. A new chapter was waiting, and I was ready to turn the page.

The weeks leading up to the move were a blur of packing boxes and shedding belongings. Each item I discarded felt like a small liberation, a step closer to a lighter existence. New Jersey had been kind to me in many ways, but it also carried the weight of a life that was no longer mine. By the time the moving van was loaded and the keys to my apartment were handed over, I felt a strange mixture of grief and exhilaration—as though I were mourning the end of an era while stepping into the unknown with arms wide open.

And so began my new chapter in LA, a city that promised nothing but demanded everything. It was the beginning of a journey not across coasts but into a version of myself I was starting to discover.

Los Angeles, often glamorized as the city of dreams, is, in reality, a place that makes no promises. Unlike cities with clear-cut paths to success, LA offers no guarantees—no assurance of stability, fame, or fulfillment. Instead, it demands relentless effort, resilience, and an almost steadfast belief in oneself.

Opportunities aren't given freely in the city; they must be carved out, often at great personal cost. Whether in entertainment, business, or personal reinvention, LA challenges those who arrive, testing their endurance, ambition, and identity.

For me, moving to LA wasn't about a change in location—it was about stepping into the unknown, confronting the city's high demands, and discovering who I was in the process. It was the start of a transformation shaped not by what LA gave but by what it forced me to become.

The day before leaving New Jersey, my car was packed with essentials: my computer, clothes, and a few personal belongings. My neighbors surprised me with a small farewell gathering, offering kindness that touched my heart. At 3:00 a.m. in mid-December 2008, I woke, dressed, and began my three-thousand-mile journey to Los Angeles. The temperature was in the low thirties, and light rain had turned the streets into treacherous black ice. I chose a southern route across the United States, hoping to avoid snow and ice in the Midwest.

Fourteen hours into the drive, fatigue set in, and I stopped at an unpretentious motor inn north of Knoxville, Tennessee. Alone in the quiet room, doubts crept in: *What have I done? Was this a colossal mistake?* Seeking solace, I called Dr. Harris to inform her where I was and to reiterate my determination. Comforted by her words, I resolved to keep going.

The next morning, I continued my journey along the interstate, now swallowed by an unforgiving fog. It was the kind of dense, suffocating mist that erased the world around me—road signs, the center divider, even the edges of the pavement vanished into gray nothingness. I gripped the steering wheel, heart hammering and uncertain of the stretch ahead. A heavy lump of panic settled in my chest, and I could feel the slow creep of terror tightening its grip. I whispered a desperate prayer for safety, struggling to steady my breath and silence the rising dread that I might not make it through.

Memories suddenly flooded back—my dad teaching me to ride my own bike, complete with training wheels at first. He'd jog alongside me, steadying the seat with one hand and cheering me on with the other, until I no longer needed the extra wheels. I still remember the little glowing angel he mounted on my handlebars. It symbolized protection and, most importantly, my father's love for me. That angel's soft light had once lit the way for a little girl learning to trust herself. Now, years later, I longed for that same sense of security.

Then, as if summoned by my whispered prayer, two commercial transport trucks emerged from the haze, gliding side by side in perfect unison. Their towering forms and powerful headlights pierced the darkness, casting long beams through the fog like beacons. They didn't just appear—they arrived. For over two hours, I followed their glow, their pace anchoring me to something solid in a world that had gone gray and formless.

The thick fog wrapped around the car like a cocoon, hiding everything but the steady red taillights ahead. I was completely at their mercy, forced to surrender control, to trust the Light within me as well as their lights to carry me forward.

As daylight broke and visibility returned, the trucks signaled and exited the interstate, vanishing as fast as they had come. I never saw the drivers' license plates. But in the stillness of my car, I whispered a heartfelt thank you, tears pricking the corners of my eyes. They had been my silent guardians when I needed them most.

After three and a half days, navigating heavy rain in Tennessee and Arkansas and icy conditions in Arizona, I arrived in Los Angeles days before Christmas. I had followed the guiding lights—both literal and metaphorical—that led me through uncertainty of what I hoped would be a new beginning.

Amid a challenging economy, I secured a job two months after arriving in Los Angeles, becoming a Project Planner for an international cosmeceutical and nutraceutical skincare manufacturer. Reporting to top executives, I managed television launches, infomercials, and guest appearances. The role was short-lived due to the company's closure, but it gave me the means to pay off my car. Despite the setbacks I faced, I remained grateful—for my health, for Dr. Harris's support, and for the resilience and flexibility I had cultivated throughout my life.

But as the weeks turned into months, and I struggled to find stable employment in an unforgiving job market, my savings dwindled. After four months, I could no longer afford my rent. With no safety net to catch me, I found myself homeless.

It was a devastating turn—five years before I had been living in a beautiful home with Adam, a space filled with comfort and a sense of security. Now, everything was uncertain. My car became both transportation and shelter. The transition from that well-appointed life to one marked by survival was jarring, and it forced me to confront the fragility of comfort and the illusion of permanence.

Still, I did what I had always done—adapted. I reminded myself that my worth was not defined by my address, nor my value by my circumstances. Even in the midst of instability, I clung to the quiet strength I had earned over a lifetime. It wasn't the life I had imagined for myself, but it was still my life—and I was determined to survive it, one day at a time.

For eleven months, my compact sedan became my home. Though it was fully paid off, the cost of insurance and gas—small by most standards—felt monumental at the time. Having grown up in foster care, I was no stranger to instability, but living in my car brought a different kind of hardship—one that tested my spirit in new and profound ways.

During those difficult months, an old dream resurfaced—one I'd had in the fall of 2008. In the dream, I was on my hands and knees in a deep army trench. A soldier stood beside me, dressed in tan desert camouflage and heavy boots. I never saw his face, but I heard his voice. He was holding a machine gun and shielding me from danger.

"Keep your head down," he instructed.

I could hear other soldiers nearby, their voices echoing from surrounding trenches. Gunfire cracked constantly overhead. I was terrified but fixated on the soldier's boots—watching his every move, unwilling to close my eyes for fear that he might leave and I'd lose my only sense of safety. The battle seemed to last for hours.

When I awoke, I didn't understand the meaning of the dream or why I had been in that trench. I didn't know who the soldier was, but his presence left a lasting impression. In time, I came to see that dream as a form of spiritual reassurance—a reminder that even in my darkest moments I was being protected.

Days were spent seeking refuge in libraries, coffee shops, and malls, while nights unfolded in the cramped backseat of my car. At my lowest, my bank account held just $6.07. Still, help came from unexpected places. Dr. Harris quietly stepped in, sending a check along with one from a friend of hers who had heard about my situation. The combined amount was two hundred dollars. It wasn't much by most standards, but to me, it meant survival. I carefully stretched that money over several months, using it for food, gas for my car, and to keep my phone service active so I could continue our weekly therapy calls and my job search.

Those conversations with Dr. Harris helped fortify my spirit. And through it all, journaling became a daily practice in gratitude that kept me focused on the blessings I still had: my health, my endurance, and the small acts of kindness that reminded me I wasn't entirely alone.

Local libraries were more than a refuge—they became sanctuaries, offering free internet for job searches and a quiet space for reflection. One library in particular became my sanctuary—a place where I could regain my footing amid uncertainty. Its slogan, "Here for You, Every Chapter," struck a deep chord, offering a quiet yet unwavering invitation to feel a sense of belonging. Within its walls, I found more than books and resources; I found comfort and reassurance.

Even in hardship, I found solace in the beauty surrounding me—the serene Mediterranean-style architecture, the vibrant blooms that flourished year-round, and the breathtaking contrast of beaches and mountains. It was during this time that I came to understand a profound truth: Home is not a structure built on a piece of land but a state of mind. And no matter where life takes me, I carry my home within me.

Every twelve to fourteen days, I treated myself to a $40 motel room an hour west of Los Angeles, off the 101 Interstate. It became a small but essential luxury—a chance to enjoy a hot shower and a real bed, offering the much-needed rest that sustained me.

Parking at night in affluent canyon neighborhoods required careful planning. While the presence of security guards provided some comfort, I remained vigilant, arriving after sunset and leaving before dawn to avoid drawing attention.

Despite aching limbs, relentless summer heat, and the stifling confinement of my car, I fought to preserve my dignity. I navigated homelessness with inner strength and grace, refusing to let my circumstances define me. I reminded myself that everything was a state of mind. To maintain a sense of normalcy, I limited liquids after 6 p.m. to minimize restroom needs, used waterless soap for hygiene, and dressed each morning in business attire, applying makeup using my car's visor mirror. My goal was to present a polished, professional appearance to the world—proof to myself and others that I was more than my situation.

Tucked within a lush, upscale neighborhood in the foothills of the Santa Monica Mountains, a cozy coffee shop became my morning refuge. Opening its doors at 5:30 a.m., it provided more than a caffeine fix—it offered a private restroom and a quiet space to gather myself before facing the day. While A-list celebrities drifted in and out, I saw them not as icons but as individuals navigating their own journeys. And in a way, I could say I had coffee with Brian Wilson, Angie Dickinson, Paris Hilton, Leonardo DiCaprio, and Herb Alpert.

Of course, "having coffee" with them was more of an illusion. While other patrons indulged in steaming lattes, foamy cappuccinos, and breakfast platters with avocado toast and smoked salmon, I maintained my frugal ritual: a single cup of tea. Not the elaborate, fragrant kind in silk sachets—the most basic tea bag, steeped in hot water. And when the cup ran empty, I asked for more hot water, stretching the tea leaves as far as they could go.

It wasn't about saving money; it was about survival, about making the most of what little I had. A three-dollar tea was a luxury I allowed myself because it came with endless refills of warmth, a quiet corner, and an unspoken place in a world I could not afford to belong. I watched as others swiped credit cards without hesitation, their bills totaling more in a single morning than I spent in a week or more. Meanwhile, I sat in my same seat on a small sofa, hands wrapped around my teacup, savoring the comfort of something that cost nothing extra.

Despite the contrast, I never felt out of place. If anything, I had cracked the code of belonging in a world where I had no business lingering. I was not a customer; I was a fixture—one who occupied the same space as the wealthy and famous, sipping my tea while they sipped their extravagance.

In the stillness of the canyons at night, the haunting howls of coyotes reminded me of nature's raw and unrelenting presence. I took precautions, keeping food out of my car to avoid unwanted encounters. Even in these trying times, I clung to small routines and moments of peace, staying focused on rebuilding my life.

Each morning, before the sun rose and the dew settled over everything, I wiped down my car with paper towels—using the thin layer of moisture as a natural cleanser to keep it looking clean and well-kept. It wasn't just about tidiness; the appearance of my car mattered. I sought rest in upscale neighborhoods, where a spotless vehicle could blend in without raising suspicion. Looking like I belonged was crucial.

Blending into the environment wasn't just a preference—it was imperative to my survival. My car couldn't look lived in, and neither could I. I kept my clothes carefully hidden in the trunk, concealing any trace of the truth: that my car was my only shelter. My morning ritual became a quiet act of control in an otherwise uncertain world—a way to protect myself through invisibility.

One night, as I lay in my car, exhaustion tugging at me, I struggled to find rest in the uncomfortable stillness. As sleep began to take hold, the deep rumble of an engine shattered the silence. A car pulled up in front of mine, its headlights casting eerie shadows against the interior. Then came the footsteps—heavy, deliberate, closing in on my driver's side. My pulse pounded in my ears; my breath caught in my throat. I was trapped, paralyzed by fear.

In that moment, I remembered the spiritual soldier from my earlier dream. His voice, firm and resolute, echoed in my mind: *Stay down. Never lift your head.* It was not a memory—it felt as though he was there with me, his presence strong and protective. I obeyed, lying motionless under a bath towel and some extra clothes, willing myself to become invisible.

Minutes stretched into hours as I remained hidden in the darkness, my body rigid with tension. Every creak of the night, every rustle of wind against the car, felt amplified—each one a potential threat. I hardly dared to breathe. Time lost all meaning as fear and determination held me in place.

Before dawn painted the horizon in soft hues, I cautiously crawled into the front seat, my limbs stiff from staying still so long. I turned the key in the ignition, the engine breaking the silence like a gunshot. Ahead of me, the driver in the other car jolted upright, startled. I saw the flicker of confusion in their rearview mirror as they glanced back—realizing, perhaps for the first time, that I had been there all along.

But I didn't wait for questions or confrontation. I eased onto the road and disappeared before they could react. Relief surged through me, warm and overwhelming. I was safe. Gratitude swelled in my chest—for the unseen spiritual protection that had held me through the long, harrowing night and guided me into the light.

That soldier—my guardian angel—became more than a fleeting vision. He was a symbol of protection, a force that carried me through the danger of my year of homelessness. Whether real or imagined, his presence reminded me that I was protected. He was there, standing guard, ensuring I survived.

But sometimes, when I closed my eyes and tried to remember his face, a thought would stir quietly within me: Was Chalay the soldier? The question echoed in the stillness, unanswered but persistent. There was something familiar in his strength, something comforting in the way he appeared when I was most afraid. I couldn't explain it, but his presence felt divine. Like someone who knew my pain. Someone who loved me across time and space.

Maybe it didn't matter if he was flesh and blood or spirit. What mattered was that in my darkest moments, he was there. Watching. Protecting. And that was enough to keep me going.

Job hunting was as grueling as finding safe places to park my car each night. Employment gaps and age bias worked against me. Though I maintained my health, youthful appearance, and active lifestyle, interviewers often dismissed me as "too old." Background checks revealed my date of birth, reinforcing their assumptions.

To counter biases, I emphasized my leadership skills, showcasing achievements in project management, human resources, and operations. I drew on my experience with international clients and community organizations to position myself as a seasoned professional capable of driving growth and delivering results.

After a year of relentless searching and scraping by, I finally landed a job as Operations Manager for a nationwide debt management company. The salary was modest, but to me, it felt like salvation—my first real step toward stability. It was enough to rent a small spare bedroom from a kind woman in an upscale neighborhood, who was nursing her own wounds from a recent divorce. We were both quietly rebuilding our lives, each in our own way.

Reporting directly to the company's president, I took on a wide range of responsibilities: overseeing daily operations, managing staff, developing internal policies, and maintaining relationships with clients. It was a demanding role, but I embraced it with gratitude and determination. After everything I had endured, having purpose again—and a door to close behind me at night—felt like a gift.

The role provided much-needed financial relief but came with a heavy burden. The company operated without a license, employed undocumented workers, and required staff to use fictional names. I carried out my assigned duties during the day, all while witnessing firsthand the corruption that ran through the business. Though necessity kept me there, I refused to turn a blind eye. At my apartment in the evenings, I recorded violations and reported them to local, state, and federal authorities. Each day felt like walking a tightrope—fulfilling my job responsibilities while working to expose the truth.

In 2013, after two and a half years, state and federal authorities shut the company down. As I drove home on my last day, the secrecy and corruption that had hung over the workplace finally lifted—only to be replaced by the stark reality of unemployment. The silence that followed was heavy, but it also held space for something new.

That night, I had a dream.

I was sitting at a table on the patio outside the small rented bedroom where I lived. A small bird fluttered toward me, hovering in the air before landing gently in my open hands. At first, it was tense and hesitant, as if unsure whether it could trust me. But after a moment, it relaxed, nestling into my palms with a quiet confidence.

Without a single word spoken, I understood her message. She was female, round and full—ready to bring new life into the world. I could feel her strength, her determination, her deep sense of readiness. And then, through a kind of intuitive knowing, she spoke—not in language but in meaning: *You, too, are close to starting a new life.*

It was a beautiful and powerful dream. One that felt like a message from somewhere beyond my understanding, offering reassurance that I was not lost, just beginning again. I woke with a renewed sense of hope and clarity—something had shifted.

Later that day, a friend who lived nearby brought me a small gift. A fragile teacup, its surface painted with the vivid likeness of the bird from my dream. The timing, the symbol, the uncanny resemblance—it felt like an affirmation from the universe that I was indeed on the cusp of something new. A quiet reminder that even after an ending, life has a way of beginning again.

Jenna and Mark Dunmore, two extraordinary people, embraced me as family during some of the most vulnerable moments of my life. Jenna, vice president of Operations at a financial firm in Westwood, and her husband, Mark, a technical director for a hit singing competition on a major television network, became steady anchors in a world that so often felt adrift. Their unwavering support offered the encouragement I needed most.

They lived a short drive from where I was staying, and their home offered a sanctuary of warmth, comfort, and genuine love. I cherished every moment with them, our walks through their canyon neighborhood with their two beloved dogs: Sage, a dignified Rhodesian ridgeback mix with a soulful gaze, and Boone, a gentle English mastiff whose sheer size and tender heart made him unforgettable.

One evening, as Jenna and I took a walk and the sun set in a blaze of amber and gold, we paused on a steep street to take in the view. The light bathed everything around us, and without meaning to, I whispered, "Jenna, that's the face of God."

She didn't respond, and neither did I. The moment hung between us, sacred and unspoken. In California's open-minded embrace of metaphysics and spirituality, I found the courage to hold on to my own quiet truths. I had a lifelong *knowing* that I was from the Light.

When Jenna and Mark traveled to Costa Rica, they entrusted me to care for Sage and Boone. I loved being invited to stay in their home, enveloped by the peace and companionship their dogs offered. Every night, I laid out a sleeping bag in the family room so I could be close to them. Sage and Boone, with their loyal hearts and watchful eyes, flanked me on either side, their presence a shield against the world's uncertainties.

On the third night, I experienced something extraordinary. As I drifted into sleep, I felt my spirit lift from my body. I hovered above, observing myself lying there with Sage and Boone by my side. Time felt suspended, and I knew I had a choice: to remain in my spiritual form or return to my physical body.

The decision was simple. I couldn't abandon Sage and Boone, who depended on me, nor could I leave Jenna and Mark, who had opened their hearts and home to me. I returned to my body, awakening with a renewed sense of purpose. I hugged Sage and Boone, grateful for their steadfast companionship during my out-of-body experience.

That moment of separation—and the conscious decision to return—was transformative. It wasn't just an ethereal journey; it was a sacred reminder that the most profound connections in life are grounded in love, loyalty, and service. Sage and Boone were more than guardians in the night; they were divine spirits, drawing me back not through obligation but through devotion. In choosing to stay, I embraced a deeper understanding: Sometimes the greatest awakening comes not from leaving the body but from choosing to remain fully present within it.

Through every struggle—unsteady work and the ache of uncertainty— Jenna and Mark reminded me of the enduring power of human connection. They called me their "chosen family," a title I cherished more than I could express.

Even now, I hold close the memory of that little bird in my dream, her message as clear as ever: *You are close to starting a new life.* And with Jenna, Mark, Sage, and Boone by my side, I realized that new beginnings were not a promise—they were a reality waiting to unfold.

A year later, I began part-time consulting for the founder of an international skincare company. While the work was fulfilling, the lack of steady income forced me into bankruptcy. The process was grueling, but it marked a turning point—a chance to close one chapter and begin anew.

In July 2014, I joined a family-owned food processing company, tasked with overhauling its administrative practices to position the business for a profitable sale. Reporting directly to the company executives, I brought a clear, strategic vision to streamline operations and drive value across the organization.

Two weeks into the job, my first paycheck arrived. As I reviewed the check stub, I noticed an issue: While the start date was correct, my salary was short by one full day's pay. Confused, I approached the CEO's secretary, who was responsible for submitting employee hours to the bookkeeper. Her response was dismissive, claiming she had followed the CEO's explicit instructions. Frustration mounting, I escalated the matter to the bookkeeper via email, requesting a review and resolution. I expected the company to address the mistake—it seemed a basic standard of professionalism. Instead, I encountered resistance.

Determined to stay focused, I set the paycheck issue aside, though I refused to forget it. Over the next year, I implemented sweeping changes across the human resources (HR) and ordering departments. Managing a team of twenty-five, I directed HR and administrative functions for four hundred employees spread across the company's headquarters and three branch offices. What began as a consultancy role transitioned into a full-time position as Director of Human Resources and Administration within two months. I was tasked with identifying and addressing the company's unseen business needs, a challenge I took with honest enthusiasm.

My contributions didn't go unnoticed. I was rewarded with paid health insurance—a significant relief after years without coverage, even though vision and dental benefits were excluded. I rebuilt teams, recruited new talent to upgrade the skills pool, and authored a bilingual employee manual to clarify company policies and improve morale. I overhauled the company's flawed ordering system, replacing manual processes with handheld devices that increased accuracy from dismal levels to over 90 percent with a target of 100 percent in sight.

Despite these successes, the unresolved paycheck issue lingered. Each month, I revisited it with the bookkeeper, copying the CEO's secretary on all correspondence. I received reassurances that the matter would be addressed, but no action was ever taken. When a new bookkeeper was hired three months later, she acknowledged the error but still required CEO approval to process the payment—a step that never materialized.

A year into my tenure, the company merged with a larger international corporation, and my role, along with many others, was rendered redundant. Filing for unemployment once again, I also submitted a complaint for the unpaid day's wages. Six months later, after navigating an inundated system, I presented my case to the Deputy Labor Commissioner. Armed with meticulous documentation—including paycheck stubs, email correspondence, and my employment contract—I answered questions with confidence during the two-hour hearing. In the end, I was awarded compensation for the wrongdoing. The company, however, faced hefty penalties and legal consequences from the Department of Labor—a steep price for what could have been resolved with a simple correction.

Though victorious, I was unemployed once more. I confided in Dr. Harris, describing my circumstances as akin to a dark, slippery tunnel: Each time I climbed toward the light, I would slip backward, forced to start the arduous climb again. Saving during periods of employment was a priority, but those reserves were often depleted during stretches of joblessness.

Nine months later, at age sixty-three, I secured a position as Director of Operations and HR for an engineering firm experiencing rapid growth. Reporting to the president and his son, I managed operations for employees across nine locations nationwide. The company offered a relocation allowance to its headquarters in Manhattan Beach, which I promptly deposited into savings. Fearful of spending money, I completed the move using my car over several trips.

In my new role, I orchestrated the opening of a branch office in Atlanta within thirty days, negotiated vendor contracts, and implemented systems to unify operations across locations. I streamlined the contractor database and established systems for tracking insurance and business licenses, eliminating liability gaps. Despite these achievements, I soon uncovered unethical practices by the firm's leadership. These revelations shed light on the company's chronic high employee turnover.

Dr. Harris continued to advise me to search for a better opportunity. Each evening, after grueling ten to eleven hour workdays, I applied for jobs, though not a single interview came my way. By fall 2017, I was drained. Long hours and job insecurity had taken their toll, and though I never spoke of my personal challenges to colleagues, I empathized with an engineer who confided in me about his experience living on the streets before being hired.

A brief reprieve came when the founder of an international skincare boutique company, for whom I had once consulted, invited me to Tennessee to house-sit while she and her husband traveled to Hawaii. For two weeks, I stayed in her luxurious six-thousand-square-foot home, surrounded by beautiful, landscaped acres. The solitude allowed me to reconnect with myself, providing much-needed respite from the turmoil of my professional life.

When I returned to California, I walked straight into another storm. A major client severed ties with the firm after clashing with a member of the executive team, triggering a financial crisis and immediate layoffs. Five months later, I was let go. At sixty-five, I drew upon the money I had saved and invested over the years with diligence and took the courageous step of reporting the company's unethical practices to both state and federal authorities. Justice was served—the company was held accountable. Yet once again, I stood at a crossroads, facing the daunting task of forging a new path forward.

Losing jobs had become an almost predictable cycle—an exhausting pattern of instability, not because of my own shortcomings but fueled by economic collapse and the corruption woven into the fabric of the companies where I worked. Over and over again, I found myself in workplaces run by unethical leaders, forced to navigate the tension between financial necessity and moral responsibility.

The irony was glaring. I needed work, but the very people providing jobs were operating outside the law. I wasn't losing jobs—I was blowing the whistle on businesses that had no right to exist as they did. And in doing so, I was holding a mirror up to a broken system.

In the big picture of my life, this struggle was more than a string of lost jobs—it was a testament to my unwillingness to compromise integrity for the sake of a paycheck. It was the battle between survival and principle, between personal hardship and the greater good. And though uncertainty followed each loss, I had no regrets. I was doing what was right.

During my years with the engineering firm, I moved multiple times in search of stable housing. From a gated community in Manhattan Beach to various rentals in Redondo Beach, I longed for permanence and a sense of belonging. Long walks helped me maintain mental clarity amid the constant upheaval. Stability remained elusive, but my resilience carried me forward, one step at a time.

After being laid off and living on limited savings, I sought ways to cut expenses. I briefly considered returning to West LA, but an unexpected opportunity emerged—a widow offered to rent me the entire second floor of her home on the Palos Verdes Peninsula. The space included a master bedroom with an en suite bath, a walk-in closet, a small office, and a private kitchen—all for less rent than I had paid for my previous apartments. Grateful for the spacious and serene setting, I moved in under a month-to-month agreement.

Life began to feel more stable. My calls each week with Dr. Harris remained a priority, and I always prepared a list of topics to make the most of our sessions. By August 2018, twenty years into therapy, she noted that I sounded happier—a sentiment I agreed with. Despite ongoing challenges, I trusted the Light for love, safety, and guidance, finding peace in my new environment.

She and I agreed that I could now move on without our telephone conversations, but we would continue to stay in touch. I was fortunate to have found her and to benefit from her time and generosity. Dr. Harris never charged me for the twenty years that she worked with me. She knew I was in a crisis situation and extended her expertise and compassion to guide me through the ups and downs of a wild emotional roller coaster ride.

From my rental, I enjoyed sweeping panoramic views of the Pacific Ocean. Sunrises and sunsets became profound spiritual experiences, deepening my connection to the Light. Each morning at 5:00 a.m., I hiked up the canyon for a meditative speed walk. The trails offered breathtaking views and encounters with foxes, coyotes, raccoons, ravens, and peacocks. Those walks were sacred to me, a time for reflection and spiritual renewal.

In my meditative state, I felt weightless, as though floating through the canyon. The physical exertion of the hike faded, replaced by a sense of transcendence. Returning to my rental, I felt a renewed sense of purpose and gratitude for the beauty and resilience of life, both in nature and within myself.

A few days before Thanksgiving 2019, I awoke during the morning hours to a luminous sphere hovering above my chest. The glowing orb, about the size of a large grapefruit, seemed to radiate a protective energy. When I shifted onto my right side, the sphere moved with me, maintaining its position beside my chest. Turning onto my left side, I noticed the sphere followed once again. Though unable to comprehend the significance of this phenomenon, I came to understand its remarkable and protective meaning within days.

After Thanksgiving, I helped my housemate, Sylvia, prepare for the Christmas holidays and looked forward to celebrating my sixty-seventh birthday on Christmas Eve with her family and friends. Decorating her home brought joy, even as fatigue crept in. I adorned the staircase with gold garland, multicolored lights, ornaments, and tartan ribbon bows, immersing myself in the festive spirit.

Days later, I woke up feeling tired and achy, assuming I had the seasonal flu. Despite mild symptoms, I continued my walks through the canyon. However, as the days passed, my fever, chills, sore throat, and coughing worsened, forcing me to retreat from Sylvia's holiday gatherings. Too ill to speak, I communicated via text and email while Sylvia brought homemade chicken soup to my room. By the first week of January 2020, my symptoms had escalated—coughing fits, chest pain, and extreme fatigue left me unable to perform even simple tasks.

I visited an emergency clinic, where I noticed many sick patients who had disembarked from a cruise ship at the nearby Port of Long Beach. After a two-hour wait, the doctor prescribed a four-day antibiotic treatment. I began to recover and resumed my speed walking routine by the end of January. My health insurance covered most of my medical expenses, and I felt immense gratitude for my full recovery. Reflecting on the luminous sphere of light I had encountered weeks earlier, I now saw it as a sign of protection during my illness.

As I looked back on January through March of 2020, I realized my symptoms aligned with COVID-19, though I was diagnosed with severe bronchitis before the pandemic's onset. California confirmed its first COVID-19 cases in late January and declared a state of emergency in March. While the lockdowns disrupted lives worldwide, I found solace in my morning walks, grateful for the peace they brought. The year 2020 remains unforgettable—a time of resilience and reflection amid global upheaval.

The pandemic deepened my spiritual connection to the Divine—everything past, present, and future. I felt a profound sense of unity with all creation, transcending borders, wealth, and status. This heightened awareness filled me with empathy and compassion for every being, strengthening my sense of interconnectedness and solidarity.

It also deepened my awareness of life's impermanence. Each morning, as I walked in quiet reflection, I questioned my purpose. With no family to anchor me and no job to define me, one might assume I would feel untethered, ready to let go. Yet, something within me resisted. Though my circumstances were challenging, I found myself asking for more time in this human form—not out of fear but from a profound and unexplainable pull to continue serving in this realm. It was as if my work here was unfinished, though I couldn't yet see the full picture.

In those moments of self-reflection, I leaned into the guiding Light, trusting that it would reveal the path ahead. And in that trust, I found clarity, comfort, and an unexpected sense of peace.

I felt gratitude for my simple, organized life. While others decluttered during lockdown, I appreciated already living with what I needed or cherished, free from the burden of excessive possessions. This simplicity allowed me to focus on what mattered.

Though restrictions limited me, I found joy in nature's beauty, birdsong, kind neighbors, and the unconditional love of neighborhood dogs. Their pure affection reminded me of life's essence.

The pandemic reaffirmed my resilience and my enduring connection to the Light, which has guided me through adversity. This profound spiritual transformation continues to shape my perspective and actions as I navigate the physical world.

In October 2020, five months after California's stay-at-home order, I received a call from a former colleague from the engineering firm where I had served as Director of Operations and HR. He was launching his own engineering business and asked me to assist as a human resources consultant to recruit and retain staff for his new nationwide company. Though cautious about the risks of working for a start-up, I agreed, drawn by our shared passion for our fields. At sixty-seven, I was eager to remain productive and build my savings, appreciating the flexibility to work from home.

The turning point in my journey toward peace and stability came through deep self-reflection, spiritual experiences, and the firm support of key figures in my life. A pivotal moment was realizing that everything is a state of mind—an understanding that allowed me to shift my perspective and reclaim my self-worth. Dr. Harris, who provided me with consistent emotional support and therapy for two decades, played a crucial role in my healing. My father's profound lessons, his belief in my strength and self-sufficiency, echoed throughout my life, helping me break free from the past and build a foundation of resilience, inner peace, and stability.

In June 2021, I confided in a friend about a quiet longing that had taken root in my heart—the desire to welcome a beagle into my life. What I didn't mention at first was that, deep down, my heart yearned for another bloodhound. Their expressive eyes, pendulous ears, and steadfast loyalty had left a permanent mark on my soul. There is nothing like the presence of a bloodhound—majestic and soulful.

I knew the commitment it took to care for a bloodhound: the physical strength to handle a 125-pound dog who could catch a scent and bolt like lightning, and the large, secure fenced-in property that allows them a safe area to exercise. Neither of these were part of my current reality.

Still, the longing remained. So, I shifted my perspective. What if I could capture the spirit of a bloodhound in a more manageable package? That's when the beagle came to mind.

I was searching for a true companion—someone to bring lightness to my days, inspire movement, and renew my sense of purpose. And though I may have traded in the deep bellow of a bloodhound for the melodic bay of a beagle, I found what I needed: a devoted little soul to walk beside me, sniffing out happiness wherever we could find it.

By a beautiful twist of fate, my friend connected me with a woman in Canada who had a litter of beagle puppies. As I watched videos and scrolled through the photos she shared, one tri-colored pup captured my heart. There was something about his joyful spirit that made time stand still. He reminded me of my first beagle, Millie—the same expressive eyes, the same quiet depth.

But this connection went deeper than a resemblance. This pup radiated a kind of uncontainable energy and zest for life that was a reflection of my own spirit. In that instant, I knew with certainty—he was the one. I named him Mason, a name that, to me, symbolizes strength, loyalty, and heartfelt devotion.

Born in July 2021, Mason became part of my life in late October when his owner flew with him to San Diego to meet me at a convention that we were both attending. At twelve weeks old, he handled the journey with remarkable calm, snoozing in his airline carrier. The moment I met him, I felt something shift—his vibrant energy and love filled a space in me that had been empty.

Around that same time, I began reflecting on my own path. Remote work had given me the freedom to reconsider where I wanted to live. California, once my sanctuary, no longer felt like home. The state had changed, but so had I. The rising cost of living and shifting dynamics highlighted the deeper transformation within me. I realized that the happiness I sought wasn't tied to a location but to an inner sense of peace. With Mason by my side, I embraced the idea of starting anew—wherever the Light guided me.

Encouraged by friends in the Mid-Atlantic, I chose to relocate to Maryland, where I could be closer to a supportive community. A month after bringing Mason home, I packed my belongings, trusting the intuitive Light within me to guide this leap of faith. The three-thousand-mile journey was smooth, thanks in part to Mason's quick adjustment to housebreaking and his contentment traveling in his carrier fastened in the backseat.

After three and a half days on the road, we arrived in Maryland before Thanksgiving. Finding a home there felt orchestrated, as intuitive nudges and synchronicities led me to a welcoming community of kindred spirits. Nestled in a neighborhood surrounded by trees and walking trails, I felt an immediate sense of peace. Kind neighbors, vibrant seasons, and the quiet beauty of the Mid-Atlantic affirmed that I was where I was meant to be.

Mason thrived in our new environment, his playful energy drawing me outdoors for long walks along wooded paths and serene parks. Together, we explored our surroundings, deepening our bond with each shared experience.

This move marked more than a geographical transition—it was a spiritual one. It reminded me that the Light within me, ever-present and unwavering, had guided me here for my growth and highest good, as it had carried me through childhood struggles, family hardships, and life's uncertainties. In time, I came to understand that transitions are not meant to be feared but embraced—as necessary steps in the ever-unfolding, beautiful journey of life.

Conclusion

My story began as a frightened, uncertain child, lost in a world that felt vast and indifferent. Each day was a battle for belonging, a struggle to find something solid in a life built on constant change. The streets I walked were cold; the walls around me felt insurmountable. Yet, somewhere in the depths of my uncertainty, I unearthed a truth: Survival wasn't about resistance—it was about resilience.

I learned early that resilience isn't born from comfort but forged in challenge. What once seemed like an impossible future, too distant to grasp, became the foundation for a journey of strength. With every fall, I came to understand that true resilience isn't measured by the hardships we avoid but by our ability to rise each time we are knocked down.

There is a story about an underdog, overlooked and bruised, who defied every expectation. That story is Seabiscuit's. A small racehorse, dismissed by many as unremarkable, he rose beyond the odds to become a legend. Though most saw weakness, a few recognized his hidden potential. In their unwavering faith, he found the strength to overcome every challenge, proving that even in our lowest moments, greatness is still within reach.

I often think of Seabiscuit's story, for it resonates with my own. Like that underdog, I began my journey with a foundation far from perfect. Yet, just as he found his stride against all expectations, I, too, discovered the strength to rise.

My childhood, marked by the instability of foster homes, rejection, and emotional abandonment, left me feeling broken—like a puzzle with missing pieces. There were times when everything I longed for—belonging, peace, and a sense of purpose—seemed too distant to even imagine. Yet, through the darkness, I found a flicker of hope: a belief that no matter how battered life may seem, there is always the possibility for healing, for transformation, for something greater. I carried with me the conviction that you don't throw away a life just because it's been hurt. And that belief became my anchor in the storm.

Resilience is not a trophy, nor a final destination—it is a process, a way of being. It is a quiet strength that grows from every challenge, from every setback. It is in the small moments when you choose to keep moving forward, even when the way is unclear and the weight of the world feels too heavy. Resilience is in the decision to forgive, to trust again, to try once more. Every heartbreak, every failure, every tear has become a thread woven into the fabric of who I am. The scars I carry no longer symbolize the pain of the past; instead, they are reminders of the strength that grew in response to it.

Gratitude has been my constant companion. This gratitude does not erase the hardship, nor does it ignore the tears that were shed. But it allows me to honor the lessons learned through struggle. I am grateful for the people who stayed, for the ones who believed in me when I couldn't see my own worth, and for the clarity that emerged from the chaos. Through this gratitude, I transformed a story of survival into a celebration of growth, healing, and purpose. I learned to honor the journey, not just the destination.

As I neared the final stages of publishing this memoir, I had a dream that illuminated this journey in a way only dreams can. I found myself in a serene, sunlit field, the air heavy with peace and golden light. My father sat beside me, his presence grounding me with a love that transcended words. His arm rested across my shoulders, steady and warm, like the unshakable support I had always needed.

"I want to be with you," I said, my heart full of longing.

His familiar smile softened his face as he replied, "I am with you."

"But I always want you to be with me," I pressed, afraid of losing this moment.

With a voice that carried the weight of truth, he said, "I will always be with you."

At that moment, a wave of peace washed over me. His words were not just a promise but a truth that resonated within me. I woke with a renewed sense of certainty, as though my father's eternal presence had illuminated the path before me.

Reflecting on that dream, I am reminded of the teachings of the Tao Te Ching, which reveal the interconnectedness of all things and the eternal nature of the universe. My father's presence is not confined to memory or spirit—it is part of the infinite current of existence. Just as the Tao flows through all things, so, too, does his love, wisdom, and strength continue to guide me.

To you, dear reader, I offer this: Your story is still unfolding. Every chapter, no matter how painful, holds the power to transform you. The challenges you face are not walls but steppingstones on your path to becoming more than you ever dreamed possible. You are the author of your life. The power to rewrite, reshape, and rise is within you. Embrace it.

As this chapter of my life draws to a close, I step into the future with hope, courage, and curiosity. The frightened child who once stepped into the unknown has uncovered a well of inner strength that can never be taken away. There will be new challenges ahead, but there will also be new victories, joys, and lessons. The journey continues, as it always does, and with each step, I am reminded of the boundless possibilities that lie ahead.

Celebrate your resilience, honor your journey, and never stop believing in the power within you. Life may bring its storms, but together, we are proof that we can always find our way into the Light. And through it all, love—like the Tao—is always present, always whole.

Today, I choose to use the lessons of my journey to walk beside others who find themselves in dark places. Through my writing, mentoring, and advocacy, I hope to remind others that their stories, too, can be rewritten, not defined by suffering but transformed by resilience. If even one reader finds strength, comfort, or hope in these pages, then the pain I endured has found its purpose.

Acknowledgments

Writing this memoir has been a profound journey of self-discovery, offering moments of deep reflection, emotional healing, and immense gratitude. It has allowed me to honor the remarkable people and transformative experiences that shaped me into the resilient person I am today.

To my late father, whose wisdom, confidence, and love laid the foundation for me to navigate the world with strength and courage. Your belief in my potential, even when I doubted myself, gave me the courage to face challenges head-on. Your faith became my anchor, and your encouragement echoes in every achievement of mine. Though our time together was far too short, the spiritual bond we share transcends time and remains a guiding light in my life.

To my deceased mother, I offer my gratitude in a heartfelt and unconventional way. Your struggles with prescription drug dependency taught me invaluable lessons about self-awareness, resilience, and the importance of making healthy choices. These lessons have shaped my path, and for that, I honor you and the strength I gained from your challenges.

To my departed older sister, who faced mental health issues and learning disabilities with courage and heart. Though you could not fulfill the traditional role of a big sister, your love, laughter, and presence were immeasurable. We endured bullying and hardships together, and those shared experiences strengthened our bond in ways I will always treasure. Your kindness and generosity touched everyone who knew you, and the gifts you gave me are lasting reminders of your beautiful spirit.

To Dr. Rachel Harris, PhD, a true miracle in my life. Your unwavering compassion and steadfast guidance over two decades gave me the tools to understand my experiences and the strength to heal. You helped me transform pain into purpose, and your impact on my life has been nothing short of lifesaving. I will always carry your wisdom with me.

I extend my deepest gratitude to Kathleen Groom, Founder of Book Journey LLC, whose vision, expertise, and unwavering support guided this memoir from concept to creation with both professionalism and grace. My heartfelt thanks to her exceptional team—April Rust, editorial project manager; Michelle Miller, proofreader; Alli King, website designer; and Deborah Stocco and Erin Stocco, cover designer and formatter—for your meticulous care, creativity, and steadfast belief in my story. Each of you played a vital role in shaping this book with precision, integrity, and heart, helping transform deeply personal experiences into a work I am proud to share with the world.

In bringing my broader vision to life, I also wish to express my sincere appreciation to Tom Deja of Bossman Graphics for his exceptional graphic design work in creating the logo for my company, Rise and Resilience, LLC. His creative insight and thoughtful attention to detail translated my mission into a visual identity that powerfully reflects strength, healing, and transformation. The logo stands as a meaningful symbol of the work I am called to do, and his contribution remains an enduring part of this journey, both personally and professionally.

To Laura Hillenbrand, author of *Seabiscuit: An American Legend,* your extraordinary storytelling reminded me that even those deemed broken can rise above challenges to achieve greatness. Your words inspired me to embrace my own journey with resilience and to share my story with the hope that it might inspire others as yours inspired me.

Finally, to every foster child, to anyone who has ever felt unseen or abandoned, and to those living with mental illness or learning disabilities: This book is for you. My story is a testament to the resilience within us all and a reminder that hope is always within reach. You are never alone.

With heartfelt gratitude,

Cynthia Goble

About the Author

Cynthia Goble is an accomplished leader whose career spans startups, international ventures, nonprofits, and Fortune 500 companies. Known for her innovative thinking, collaborative leadership, and steadfast commitment to ethics and transparency, she has earned respect across diverse industries. As an author, motivational speaker, and founder of Rise and Resilience, LLC, she empowers others to navigate adversity with courage, clarity, and purpose.

Beyond her professional life, Cynthia is a devoted advocate for animal welfare and a proud bloodhound enthusiast. She supports rescue efforts, volunteers with breed organizations, and is rarely without one of her beloved bloodhounds snuggled nearby.

With *Forever A Foster Child*, Cynthia hopes to offer a testament to the strength of the human spirit and to inspire readers toward healing, resilience, and transformation.